CW01395211

BEDTIME STORIES FOR ADULTS

RELAXING SLEEP STORIES FOR EVERYDAY GUIDED MEDITATION. DEEP SLEEP HYPNOSIS TO FALL ASLEEP FAST AND PREVENT ANXIETY/PANIC ATTACKS. LETTING GO AND REDUCE STRESS FOR GROWN-UPS

BY

Kelly Joyful

5

THE TWELVE BROTHERS

Once upon a time there was a king and a queen who lived in peace with each other and had twelve children, but these were all boys. Now the king said to his wife, "If the thirteenth child you give birth is a girl, then the twelve boys are to die so that his wealth may be great and the kingdom falls to him alone." He also had twelve coffins made they were already filled with wood shavings, and in each lay the pillow of the dead, and had them brought into a locked room, then he gave the key to the queen and told her not to tell anyone about it.

The mother, however, sat all day long and mourned, so that the smallest son, who was always with her, and whom she called Benjamin after the Bible, said to her: "Dear mother, why are you so sad?" - "Dearest Child, "she replied," I can not tell you. "But he did not leave her any peace until she left and unlocked the room and showed him the twelve shots filled with wood shavings. Then she said, "My dearest Benjamin, these coffins have been made by your father for you and your eleven brothers, for if I give birth to a girl, then you shall all be killed and buried in it." And when she cried while she was that said, the son consoled her and said: "Do not cry, dear mother, we will help ourselves already and will go away." But she said: "Go out into the forest with your eleven brothers, and one always sits down on the tallest tree that can be found and keep watch and look for the tower here in the castle. If I give birth to a son, I will put on a white flag, and then you may return; if I give birth to a little daughter, I will put on a red flag, and then flee away as fast as you can, and God help you. Every night I want to get up and pray for you, in winter, that you can warm yourself by a fire, in summer, that you do not languish in the heat. " as fast as you can, and God help you. Every night I want to get up and pray for you, in winter, that you can warm yourself by a fire, in summer, that you do not languish in the heat. " as fast as you can, and

Bedtime Stories for Adults & For Kids

57 Mindfulness Meditations Stories to Help You and your Children Fall Asleep Fast and Overcome Insomnia & Anxiety, Best Self Healing Tales to Feel Calm Now

BY:
Kelly Joyful

TABLE OF CONTENTS
BEDTIME STORIES

God help you. Every night I want to get up and pray for you, in winter, that you can warm yourself by a fire, in summer, that you do not languish in the heat. "

After blessing their sons, they went out into the forest. One man stopped at the other, sat on the tallest oak, and looked for the tower. When eleven days were around and the turn came to Benjamin, he saw how a flag was put on. It was not the white, but the red blood flag that proclaimed that they should all die. As the brothers heard this, they became angry and said, ' Should we suffer death for the sake of a girl! We swear we want to take revenge. Where we find a girl, let his blood flow. "

Then they went deeper into the forest, and in the middle of it, where it was darkest, they found a little cursed little house, empty. Then they said, "Here we want to live and you, Benjamin, you are the youngest and weakest, you should stay home and keep household, we others want to go out and get food." Now they went into the woods and shot rabbits, wild deer, Birds and little boys, and whatever food they had, they brought to Benjamin, who had to prepare them so that they could satisfy their hunger. In the little house they lived together for ten years, and the time did not last long.

The little daughter who had given birth to her mother, the queen, had now grown up, was kind-hearted and beautiful, and had a golden star on her forehead. Once, when the laundry was big, he saw twelve men's shirts und asked his mother: "To whom do these twelve shirts belong, but are they too small for the father?" Then she answered with a heavy heart: "Dear child, these are your twelve Brothers. "The girl said," Where are my twelve brothers? I have never heard of them. "She replied," God knows where they are. They are wandering around the world. "Then she took the girl and unlocked the room for him, showing him the twelve coffins with the shavings and the dead pillow. "These coffins," she said, "were meant for your brothers, but they secretly departed before you were born, "And told him how everything had happened. Then the girl said: "Dear mother, do not cry, I want to go and look for my brothers."

Now it took the twelve shirts and went away and straight into the big forest. It went on all day and in the evening it came to the cursed house. Then he came in and found a young boy who asked, "Where are you from and where do you want to go?" And was astonished that she was so beautiful, wearing royal clothes and a star on her forehead. Then she answered, "I am a princess of the king, seeking my twelve brothers, and I will go as far as the sky is blue until I find them." She also showed him the twelve shirts that belonged to them. Then Benjamin saw that it was his sister and said, "I am Benjamin, your youngest brother." And she began to cry for joy, and Benjamin also, and they kissed and caressed each other with great love. Afterwards he said: "Dear sister, there is still a reservation, we had arranged that every girl we met would die because we had to leave our kingdom for a girl. "She said," I would like to die if I can save my twelve brothers. "-" No. "He answered," you shall not die, sit down under this tub until the eleven brothers come, then I will already be in agreement with them. "So she did; and as night came the others came from the hunt, and the meal was ready. And as they sat at the table eating, they asked, "What's new?" Benjamin said, "Do you know nothing?" - "No," they answered. He continued: "You have been in the forest, and I have stayed at home, and yet know more than you." - "Tell us," they cried. He answered, "Do you promise me that the first girl we meet, shall not be killed? "-" Yes, "cried they all," that shall have mercy, tell us only! "Then he said," Our sister is here, "and opened the chest, and the king's daughter came forth, in Her royal dress with the golden star on her forehead, and was so beautiful, delicate and fine. Everyone was happy, they fell around their necks and kissed them and loved them dearly.

Now she stayed with Benjamin at home and helped him at work. The elves moved into the forest, catching scavengers, deer, birds, and little pigeons to eat, and the sister and Benjamin made sure it was cooked. She sought the wood for cocking and the herbs for the vegetables and put the pots to the fire, so that the meal was always ready when the elves came. She also kept order in the little house, and covered the bedclothes pretty white and pure, and the brothers were always content and lived in great unity with her.

At one time the two of them had made a nice meal at home, and as they were all together, they sat down, ate and drank, and were full of joy. But it was a small garden at the cursed house, in it were twelve lily flowers, which are also called students. Now she wanted to give her brothers a treat, broke off the twelve flowers and thought of giving each one a meal. But as she had broken the flowers, at that moment the twelve brothers were transformed into twelve ravens and flew across the forest, and the house with the garden was also gone. There the poor girl was alone in the wild forest, and as it turned around, an old woman stood beside him, saying, "My child, what did you start? Why did not you leave the twelve white flowers? These were your brothers, who are now forever changed into ravens. "The girl said, crying," Is not there any way to redeem her? "-" No, "said the old woman," there is none in the whole world, as But it is so difficult that you will not liberate them, because you have to be silent for seven years, you cannot speak and you cannot laugh, and you speak one word, and only one hour is missing at the seven years, so it's all in vain, and your brothers are killed by the one word. "

Then the girl said in his heart, "I know for certain that I deliver my brethren," and went and sought a tall tree, sat on it, and spun, and did not speak, and did not laugh. Now it happened that a king was hunting in the forest, he had a big greyhound who ran to the tree where the girl was sitting on it, jumped around, screamed and barked up. Then came the king, and beheld the beautiful princess with the golden star on his forehead, and was so delighted with her beauty, that he cried out to her if she wished to become his wife. She did not answer, but nodded her head slightly. Then he himself climbed the tree, carried it down, put it on his horse, and brought her home. Then the wedding was celebrated with great splendor and joy; but the bride did not speak and did not laugh. When they had lived together for a few years, the mother of the king, who was a wicked woman, began to slander the young queen, and said to the king, "It is a mean mendicant girl that you have brought with you, who knows. What ungodly pranks she secretly drives. If she is dumb and can not speak, she might laugh, but he who does not laugh has a guilty conscience. "The king did not want to believe it at first, but the old woman did it for so long and accused her of so many bad things that the king was finally persuaded and sentenced to death. What ungodly pranks she secretly drives. If she is dumb and can not speak, she might laugh, but he who does not laugh has a guilty conscience. "The king did not want to believe it at first, but the old woman did it for so long and accused her of so many bad things that the king was finally persuaded and sentenced to death. What ungodly pranks she secretly drives. If she is dumb and can not speak, she might laugh, but he who does not laugh has a guilty conscience. "The king did not want to believe it at first, but the old woman did it for so long and accused her of so many bad things that the king was finally persuaded and sentenced to death.

Now a big fire was lit in the yard, and it was to be burned in it. And the king stood at the top of the window, watching with crying eyes because he still loved her so much. And when she was already tied to the stake and the fire licked her clothes with red tongues, the last moment of the seven years had just passed. There was a clatter in the air, and twelve ravens came and lowered themselves. And as they touched the earth, it was their twelve brothers that had redeemed them. They tore the fire apart, extinguished the flames, released their dear sister, and kissed and caressed her. But now that she was allowed to open her mouth and speak, she told the king why she had been dumb and never laughed. The king was happy when he heard that she was innocent, and they all lived together in unity until her death. The wicked stepmother was put on trial and put in a cask filled with boiling oil and venomous snakes, and died a wicked death.

FROM THE FISHERMAN AND HIS WIFE

Once upon a time there was a fisherman and his wife, who lived together in a small fisherman's hut, close to the sea, and the fisherman went every day fishing and fishing and fishing.

So he once sat with his fishing rod and always looked into the clear water: and so he sat and sat.

Then the rod went down to the bottom, and when he raised it, he brought out a big butt. Butt said to him, "Look, fisherman, I beg you, let me live, I'm not a real butt, I'm a haunted prince. What's the use of killing me? I would not like you right: Put me back in the water and let me swim. "-" Well, "said the man," you do not need to say so many words: a butt who can speak, I will probably swim Let him put it back in the clear water. The butt went to the bottom and left a long strip of blood behind. Then the fisherman got up and went to his wife in the little hut.

"Man," said the woman, "have you caught anything today?" - "No," said the man. "I caught a butt who said he was a haunted prince, so I let him swim again." - "Did not you wish for anything?" Said the woman. "No," said the man, "what should I wish for?" - "Oh," said the woman, "that is bad to always dwell here in the hut: it stinks and is so disgusting; You could have wished us a little house. Go back and call him. Tell him we want to have a little house, he certainly does. "-" Oh, "said the man," what should I go there again? "-" I, "said the woman," you had caught him and let him swim again - he certainly does. Go straight! "The man did not want to be right,

When he got there, the sea was quite green and yellow and not so clear anymore. So he stood and said:

12

"Little Man, Little Man, Timpe Te,

Buttje, Buttje in the Sea,

My wife, the Ilsebill,

Will not do what I want."

"Well, what does she want?" Said the butt. "Oh," said the man, half saddened, "she wants to live in a big stone castle." - "Go on, she's at the door," said the butt.

Then the man went and thought that he wanted to go home, but when he came there, there stood a big stone palace, and his wife stood on the top of the stairs and wanted to go in: then she took him by the hand and said: "Just come in." With that he went in with her, and in the castle was a large hallway with a marble screed, and there were so many servants, they tore open the big doors, and the walls were all bare and with beautiful wallpaper and in the rooms were nothing but golden chairs and tables, and crystal chandeliers hung from the ceiling; all rooms and chambers were provided with floor coverings. On the tables stood the food and the very best wine that they almost wanted to break. And behind the house was a large yard with a horse and cowshed, and a carriage: everything of the very best; there was also a large, beautiful garden with the most beautiful flowers and fine fruit trees, and a splendid park, probably half a mile long, with deer and deer in it, and everything you could wish for. "Well," said the woman, "is not that beautiful?" "Oh, yes," said the man, "that's the way it should be. Now we also want to live in the beautiful castle and want to be satisfied. "-" We want to remember that, "said the woman," and want to sleep it. "Then they went to bed.

The next morning the woman woke up first; It had just become day, and from her bedside she saw the glorious land before her. The man still stretched when she elbowed him in the side and said, "Man, get up and look out of the window. See, can not we become king over all the land? Go to the Butt, let us be King. "" Oh, woman, "said the man," why do we want to be king? "" Well, "said the woman," if you do not want to be king, I will be king , Go to the Butt, I will be King. "" Oh, woman, "said the man," what do you want to be king? I do not want to tell him that. "-" Why not? "Said the woman," go straight, I must be king. "Then the man went away, and was very depressed that his wife wanted to become king. That's not right, the man thought.

And when he came to the sea, the sea was all black-gray, and the water was rushing up from below and stinking lazily. So he stood and said:

> *"Little Man, Little Man, Timpe Te,*
>
> *Buttje, Buttje in the Sea,*
>
> *My wife, the Ilsebill,*
>
> *Will not do what I want."*

"Well, what does she want?" Said the butt. "Oh," said the man, "she wants to be king." - "Go ahead, she is already," said the butt.

Then the man went, and when he came to the palace, the castle had become much larger, with a large tower and a splendid ornament on it: and the sentry stood before the gate, and there were so many soldiers and timpani and trumpets. And when he came into the house, everything was pure marble and gold, and collected blankets and big golden tassels. Then the doors opened from the hall, where the whole court was, and his wife sat on a high throne of gold and diamonds, and had a great golden crown and the scepter in the hand of pure gold and precious stone. And on both sides of her stood six virgins in a row, always one head smaller than the other. Then he stood up and said: "O woman, are you now king?" - "Yes," said the woman, "now I am king." Then he stood and looked at her; and when he had looked at them for a while, he said, "Oh, woman, what is beautiful that you are king now! Now we do not want to wish anything more. "-" No, man, "said the woman, and was very restless," I am already for a while and I can not stand this anymore. Go to the Butt: King I am, now I must also become Emperor. "" Oh, woman, "said the man," why do you want to become Emperor? "-" Man, "she said," go to Butt, I want Be Emperor! "" Oh, woman, "said the man," he can not do the Emperor, I do not like to tell the butt that; Emperor is only once in the Reich: Emperor can not make the butt. "-" What, "said the woman," I am king, and yet you are my husband; do you want to go right now? Go straight! - If he can make kings, then he can also make emperors; I want and want to be Emperor! Go straight! "He had to go there. When the man went, he felt very anxious; and as he went away, he thought to himself, "That's not and will not work out. Kaiser is too rude, but the butt will end up feeling sorry." In the meantime he came to the sea. There the sea was still black and thick and began to foam up from below, blasting; and there was such a whirlwind over the sea that she just turned. And the man took a horror. There he stood now and said: and there was such a whirlwind over the sea that she just turned. And the man took a horror. There he stood now and said: and there was such a whirlwind over the sea that she just turned. And the man took a horror. There he stood now and said:

"Little Man, Little Man, Timpe Te,

Buttje, Buttje in the Sea,

My wife, the Ilsebill,

Will not do what I want."

"Well, what does she want?" Said the butt. "Oh, Butt," he said, "my wife wants to be Emperor." "Go on," said the butt, "she is already."

"Little Man, Little Man, Timpe Te,

Buttje, Buttje in the Sea,

My wife, the Ilsebill,

Will not do what I want."

"Well, what does she want?" Said the butt. "Oh," said the man, "she wants to be king." - "Go ahead, she is already," said the butt.

Then the man went, and when he came to the palace, the castle had become much larger, with a large tower and a splendid ornament on it: and the sentry stood before the gate, and there were so many soldiers and timpani and trumpets. And when he came into the house, everything was pure marble and gold, and collected blankets and big golden tassels. Then the doors opened from the hall, where the whole court was, and his wife sat on a high throne of gold and diamonds, and had a great golden crown and the scepter in the hand of pure gold and precious stone. And on both sides of her stood six virgins in a row, always one head smaller than the other. Then he stood up and said: "O woman, are you now king?" - "Yes," said the woman, "now I am king." Then he stood and looked at her; and when he had looked at them for a while, he said, "Oh, woman, what is beautiful that you are king now! Now we do not want to wish anything more. "-" No, man, "said the woman, and was very restless," I am already for a while and I can not stand this anymore. Go to the Butt: King I am, now I must also become Emperor. "" Oh, woman, "said the man," why do you want to become Emperor? "-" Man, "she said," go to Butt, I want Be Emperor! "" Oh, woman, "said the man," he can not do the Emperor, I do not like to tell the butt that; Emperor is only once in the Reich: Emperor can not make the butt. "-" What, "said the woman," I am king, and yet you are my husband; do you want to go right now? Go straight! - If he can make kings, then he can also make emperors; I want and want to be Emperor! Go straight! "He had to go there. When the man went, he felt very anxious; and as he went away, he thought to himself, "That's not and will not work out. Kaiser is too rude, but the butt will end up feeling sorry." In the meantime he came to the sea. There the sea was still black and thick and began to foam up from below, blasting; and there was such a whirlwind over the sea that she just turned. And the man took a horror. There he stood now and said: and there was such a whirlwind over the sea that she just turned. And the man took a horror. There he stood now and said: and there was such a whirlwind over the sea that she just turned. And the man took a horror. There he stood now and said:

"Little Man, Little Man, Timpe Te,

Buttje, Buttje in the Sea,

My wife, the Ilsebill,

Will not do what I want."

"Well, what does she want?" Said the butt. "Oh, Butt," he said, "my wife wants to be Emperor." "Go on," said the butt, "she is already."

The man was sound asleep, he had had to walk a lot during the day; but the woman could not fall asleep and threw herself from one side to the other all night, always thinking about what she might become, and could not think of anything. Meanwhile, the sun was about to rise, and when she saw the dawn, she sat upright in the bed and looked into it. And when she saw the sun coming up out of the window, Ha, she thought, can not I let the sun and the moon rise too? "Man," she said, thrusting his elbow into his ribs; "Wake up, go to the Butt, I want to be like God." The man was still drowsy, but he was so frightened that he fell out of bed. He said he had interrogated himself, rubbed his eyes and said, "Oh, woman, what do you say? "-" Man, "she said," if I can not let the sun and the moon rise, I can not stand it, and I have not a quiet hour left, that I can not let her rise. " She looked at him very angry that a shudder over him. "Go straight, I will become like the dear God." - "Oh, woman," said the man and fell on his knees in front of her, "the butt can not do that. He can do emperor and pope; - I am you, go into you and remain pope. "Then she came over the malice, her hair flew so wild around her head and she screamed:" I can not stand it! And I can not stand this anymore! Do you want to go ?! "Then he put on his pants and ran away like crazy. and I do not have a quiet hour anymore, that I can not let her go by herself. "She looked at him quite angry that a shudder over him. "Go straight, I will become like the dear God." - "Oh, woman," said the man and fell on his knees in front of her, "the butt can not do that. He can do emperor and pope; - I am you, go into you and remain pope. "Then she came over the malice, her hair flew so wild around her head and she screamed:" I can not stand it! And I can not stand this anymore! Do you want to go ?! "Then he put on his pants and ran away like crazy. and I do not have a quiet hour anymore, that I can not let her go by herself. "She looked at him quite angry that a shudder over him. "Go straight, I will become like the dear God." - "Oh, woman," said the man and fell on his knees in front of her, "the butt can not do that. He can do emperor and pope; - I am you, go into you and remain pope. "Then she came over the malice, her hair flew so wild around her head and she screamed:" I can not stand it! And I can not stand this anymore! Do you want to go ?! "Then he put on his pants and ran away like crazy. "The butt can not do that. He can do emperor and pope; - I am you, go into you and remain pope. "Then she came over the malice, her hair flew so wild around her head and she screamed:" I can not stand it! And I can not stand this anymore! Do you want to go ?! "Then he put on his pants and ran away like crazy. "The butt can not do that. He can do emperor and pope; - I am you, go into you and remain pope. "Then she came over the malice, her hair flew so wild around her head and she screamed:" I can not stand it! And I can not stand this anymore! Do you want to go ?! "Then he put on his pants and ran away like crazy.

But outside the storm went and roared that he could barely stand on his feet. The houses and the trees were blown over, and the mountains trembled, and the rocks tumbled into the sea, and the sky was pitch-black, and thundered and flashed, and the sea went in high black waves like steeples and mountains, and had all a white head of foam on top. Then he cried, and could not hear his own word:

"Little Man, Little Man, Timpe Te,

Buttje, Buttje in the Sea,

My wife, the Ilsebill,

Will not do what I want."

"Well, what does she want?" Said the butt. "Oh," he said, "she wants to be like God." - "Go on, she's back in the fisherman's hut."

They still sit there to this day.

THE LITTLE FIELD MOUSE LEARNS MAGIC

It was a lovely, balmy summer day. The little field mouse and her friends played the whole day in the field by the pond. They played catching, hiding and ran to the bet.

Suddenly the little field mouse said to her friends, "Do you know what, now I'll conjure something for you!" The friends looked at each other in astonishment. "You can do magic?" They sat on a recumbent tree trunk and watched the little field mouse in their preparations. This curled up a small stump and spread a cloth over it. On the other hand, she put a cylinder on the cloth and covered it with another cloth.

Then she raised her paws up: "Abera ca Dabera." And it happened ... nothing. The friends looked a little disappointed. The little field mouse pulled the cloth from the cylinder with a "Wusch" and reached in with his left hand. At the same time she reached down with her right hand, behind the tree stump. Then she jerked up both hands and held a small cuddly toy in her right hand. The friends applauded, but a little hesitantly.

"Um ..." said the little hedgehog, "Did you get the stuffed animal out of the cylinder? Or behind the tree stump, conjured up? "" Well, tell me! "The small field mouse was awakened. "Out of the cylinder, of course!" She asserted. "That looked different," confirmed the little frog. "Yes, exactly!" The little hedgehog again invaded. "Somehow, your 'magic' does not seem quite professional." The small field mouse lowered its head. "Yes, you are right. Actually, I can not do magic. "" Shall I teach you? "Asked the little pink piggy.

"You want to teach me magic?" Wondered the little field mouse. "Can you do that anyway?" "Klaro!" Came in response and a surprised murmur made the rounds among friends. "Show us!" Demanded the little hedgehog, who could not believe that. And the little piglet exchanged the position with the little field mouse. "Ladies and Gentlemen," it began, "now watch the famous and infamous magic show of the little pink pig!' Behavioral clapping began. The friends were not sure yet what to expect now.

"First," the magician continued, "I'll let this cuddly toy" the cuddly toy was shaken in the hand, "disappear in the cylinder!" Until now, the show did not look so bad and the little field mouse drummed with their paws a kind of drum roll on the tree trunk. The little pink piggy put the stuffed animal in the cylinder and covered it with the cloth. "Hocus and pox, the cuddly toy now disappears, but not only to the locus, but in every sense of the wind!" It waved mystically with his arms over the cylinder and pulled the cloth abruptly aside. "Ta-Taaaa!" Shouted it, putting itself in victory pose.

"Huh?" The little hedgehog let out. "The cuddly toy is still in the cylinder." "Nonsense, is not it!" Replied the pig and lifted the cylinder up and turned it around loosely Gaaaanz. When the cuddly toy should have fallen out, it did not happen. The friends got big eyes. "Where is it?" Wondered the little frog and hopped forward and examined the cylinder. In the cylinder was no cuddly toy. And there was no one behind the tree stump and the piggy had obviously no cuddly toy with him. "Hey!" Cried the little hedgehog, "you can actually do magic!" "I say!" Insisted the little pink pig.

"Then you can really teach me?" Asked the little field mouse. "Klaro!" But before that the magic show continued. "Ladies and gentlemen! Watch me spell out the cuddly toy again! "The small field mouse again made its drum roll on the tree trunk. The little frog looked at the piggy with big eyes. There's a catch, he thought, the pig CAN NOT conjure. "Aboro co Diboro! Singa Pur and Qudra Tur! Cuddly toy now come out, preferably here and not in the moor. "And again, the little piggy

21

wagged over the cylinder with the cloth on it. "TA-TAAAA!" Cried it, tore its arms up again and made the winning pose.

The clapping was a bit louder now, but stopped quickly. "I do not see it yet," the little frog grumbled again. "Should that be in the cylinder now, or what?" "Ladies and gentlemen, I'm going to turn this cylinder around slowly now." And the piggy turned the cylinder gaaaanz loosely as before. And again no cuddly toy fell out. "The cuddly toy is NOT in the cylinder. Where can it be? I've conjured it up again. "" Come on, you bang bag, tell me! "Cried the frog, who still thought it all a big scam. "My dear frog, please turn around once," said the little pink piggy.

The frog turned and saw the cuddly toy sitting on its feet behind the tree trunk on which they sat. It seemed to be smirking at the little frog. He took the cuddly toy amazed and held it up for everyone to see. And again, the pig called, "TA-TAAAAAAA!" But now the friends were clapping wildly and loud and loud. "Bravo!" "Great!" "Great!" Shouted the three spectators and the little frog patted the piggy's shoulder. "You can REALLY conjure!" And the little hedgehog rejoiced: "I know a magician! I know a magician! "

In the next few days, the little field mouse learned magic from the little pink piggy. It was not easy. It took a lot of effort to get the difficult exercises done. Some magic tricks went pretty easy. But others were really hard to learn. After a few days, she showed her friends some tricks. The friends were really excited about how well she had learned magic. They clapped, cheered and shouted for encore. At the encore, the little pink piggy had to help out a bit. But that was the best magic show the friends had ever seen and organized.

CAT AND MOUSE IN COMPANY

A cat had made acquaintance with a mouse and told her so much of the great love and friendship she bore to her that the mouse finally agreed to live with her in a house and run a communal economy. "But we have to take care of the winter, otherwise we'll be hungry," said the cat. "You, little mouse, can not venture anywhere and end up in a trap." So the good advice was followed and a potty with fat bought. But they did not know where to put it. Finally, after much deliberation, the cat said: "I know of no place where it would be better off than the church; Nobody dares to take anything away. We put it under the altar and do not touch it until we need it. "The potty was brought to safety. But it did not take long for the cat to carry cravings afterwards and say to the mouse, "What I wanted to tell you, little mouse, I've been asked by my base to be a godfather. She gave birth to a son, white with brown spots, that's what I'm supposed to say about baptism. Let me go out today and get the house alone! "-" Yes, yes, "answered the mouse," go in the name of God! If you eat something good, remember me! I also like to drink a drop of the sweet red wine! "But everything was not true. The cat had no base and was not asked to be a godfather. She went straight to the church, stole to the puddle, and licked off her fat skin. Then she went for a walk on the rooftops of the city, then stretched out in the sun and wiped her beard, whenever she thought of the puddle. It was not until evening when she came home. "Well, there you are again!" Said the mouse. "You certainly had a merry day." - "It worked," answered the cat. "What did the child get for a name?" The mouse asked. "Down," the cat said dryly. "Go on," called the mouse, "that's a strange name! Is it common in your family? "-" What's up, "said the cat. "He's no worse than Bröseldieb, as your godparents are called." "Called the mouse," that's a strange name! Is it common in your family? "-" What's up, "said the cat. "He's no worse than

23

Bröseldieb, as your godparents are called." "Called the mouse," that's a strange name! Is it common in your family? "-" What's up, "said the cat. "He's no worse than Bröseldieb, as your godparents are called."

Not long after, the cat overcame a craving again. She said to the mouse: "You must do me the favor and again get the household alone; I am asked a second time to the godfather, and since the child has a white ring around his neck, I can not refuse. "The good mouse consented, but the cat snuck behind the city wall to the church and half eaten the fat pot. "It tastes nothing better," she said, "than what you eat yourself," and was quite content with her day's work. When she came home, the mouse asked, "How was this child baptized?" - "Half way," answered the cat. "Half-Gone! What you say! I have not heard the name in my lifetime. I bet he's not on the calendar. "

The cat's mouth watered soon after the treat. "All good things come in threes," she said to the mouse. "I'm supposed to be a godfather again. The child is completely black and has only white paws, otherwise no white hair all over. This only happens once every few years. You let me go out anyway? "-" Down, half-dead, "replied the mouse," they're weird names that make me think. "-" There you sit at home in your dark gray fluffy skirt and your long hair bunny, "said the cat, "And start grilling. That's what happens if you do not go out during the day! "The mouse cleaned up during the cat's absence and fixed the house; the sweet cat, however, eats out the fat pot. "When everything is consumed, you have peace, She said to herself and came home full and fat at night. The mouse immediately asked for the name the third child had received. "He will not like you either," said the cat; "His name is Ganz." - "Whole!" Called the mouse. "That's the most public name, printed he has not yet occurred to me. All-Gone! What does that mean? "She shook her head, curled up, and went to sleep.

From now on nobody wanted to ask the cat to the godfather anymore. But when winter came and nothing was left outside, the mouse remembered its supply and said: "Come, cat, we want to go to our fat

24

pot, which we have saved ourselves! It will taste good to us. "-" Yes, "replied the cat," it will taste as if you are sticking out your fine tongue out the window. "They started out, and when they arrived, the fat pot was still standing his place, but was empty. "Oh," said the mouse, "now I realize what has happened! now it comes to the day. You are a true friend to me! You ate everything while you claimed to be a godfather: first skin off, then half off, then ... "-" Do you want to be silent! "Cried the cat. "One more word, and I'll eat you up!"

"All right," the poor mouse already had on his tongue. As soon as it was out, the cat lunged for her, grabbed her and slipped her down. You see, that's how it is in the world.

THE PRINCE IN BEARSKIN

Once upon a time there was a king who had a son. This son was very handsome, smart and knew how to handle weapons. Therefore, his father sent him to war, which he led with another kingdom. The prince, however, was abducted by hostile land and closed in a dark dungeon. One night, the prince was awakened by a strange voice. It was the devil who offered him a pact to escape from his prison. The pact read: The prince must spend three years wandering around in a terrible bearskin, and within those three years, find a girl who falls in love with him. The prince thought to himself: "I am a rich prince and there are many women who love me!" So he agreed. As a sign of the pact, the devil gave the prince a golden ring.

When the devil disappeared, the prince fell asleep and awoke in the forest the next morning. He was happy to be free and went to his castle. But the king did not recognize his son, for the prince was covered in brown hair from head to toe. So he had the beast banished from his kingdom.

The prince twisted himself back into the forest, where he hid in a small cave all summer long. When the winter came it became very cold in the cave and the prince wanted to seek refuge in a house of a gracious city dweller. He knocked cold on the doors of some houses, but when they saw the prince, they panicked the doors. He sat down on the snowy ground and wept bitterly. Then a young girl came by and immediately recognized what was hidden for a good soul and the ugly exterior. She took him home with him and nursed him well. After a while, the Prince in Bearskin said to the young woman, "Thank you for everything! But now I have to move on. I will come again! I promise!

When he had just left the house, his bearskin fell off and he was free. The young woman who cared for him was in love with him.

The prince ran home to his father, put on his best robe and drove his carriage back to his lover. But she did not recognize him. Then he gave her one half of the ring and took the girl to his castle, where they got married and lived happily ever after.

STRAW, COAL AND BEAN

In a village lived a poor old woman who had brought a dish of beans and wanted to cook them. So she made a fire on her stove, and with a handful of straw she lit it to burn faster. As she poured the beans into the pot, one unnoticed dropped her, which lay on the floor next to a straw. Soon after, a glowing coal sprang from the hearth to the two. Then the straw began, and said, "Dear friends, you come from troughs." Coal replied: "I have luckily jumped out of the fire, and if I had not enforced it by force, death was certain to me would have been burned to ashes. "The bean said," I got away with a very good skin, but if the old woman had put me in the pot, I would have been cooked to porridge without mercy, like my comrades. "-" Would I have had a better fate? "said the straw. "All my brothers have made the old woman rise in fire and smoke, sixty she has suddenly packed and killed. Fortunately, I slipped through her fingers. "-" But what should we do now? "Said the coal. "I mean," answered the bean, "because we have so happily escaped death, we will stick together as good fellows and, so that we do not meet another misfortune here, we will emigrate together and move to a foreign land." Sixty packed her and killed her. Fortunately, I slipped through her fingers. "-" But what should we do now? "Said the coal. "I mean," answered the bean, "because we have so happily escaped death, we will stick together as good fellows and, so that we do not meet another misfortune here, we will emigrate together and move to a foreign land." Sixty packed her and killed her. Fortunately, I slipped through her fingers. "-" But what should we do now? "Said the coal. "I mean," answered the bean, "because we have so happily escaped death, we will stick together as good fellows and, so that we do not meet another misfortune here, we will emigrate together and move to a foreign land."

The proposal pleased the other two, and they set off together. Soon, however, they came to a small brook, and as there was no bridge or pier there, they did not know how to get across. The straw took good advice and said, "I want to cross over, so you can walk over me like on a bridge." So the straw stretched from one shore to the other, and the coal, which was of a heated nature, also tripped very bold on the newly built bridge. But when she had come to the midst and heard the water rushing beneath her, she was afraid: she stopped and did not dare move on. The straw, however, started to burn, broke into two pieces and fell into the creek: the coal slipped, hissed as it entered the water, and gave up the ghost. The bean, who had been prudently left on the shore, had to laugh at the story, could not stop, and laughed so hard it burst. Now it had happened to them too, if not for good luck a tailor, who was on the move, would have rested at the brook. Because he had a compassionate heart, he took out needle and thread and sewed it together. The bean thanked him very well, but since he had used black twine, since then all the beans have a black seam. Because he had a compassionate heart, he took out needle and thread and sewed it together. The bean thanked him very well, but since he had used black thread, since then all beans have a black seam. Because he had a compassionate heart, he took out needle and thread and sewed it together. The bean thanked him very well, but since he had used black thread, since then all beans have a black seam.

THE DANISH KING

Denmark is high up north, where Germany stops. There is still a king there today, but he is no longer there to govern, but usually visits kindergartens because his wife likes children so much.

But a long time ago, the Danish king was very powerful. As all kings used to do, he always wanted to increase his land so that he would become even more powerful. So he also had to conquer another country. That was not easy. In the south of Denmark was Germany, then the kingdoms of Hanover and Prussia. He could not mess with them because they had many more soldiers than he. Likewise the Swedes, whose country lies next to Denmark.

So he looked north. Far behind the sea was Greenland. This is a huge country, but at the time it was very little known and it was supposed to be very cold there. So he had three ships loaded from the royal fleet. On each he put a brave knight and several soldiers, as well as horses and all kinds of war equipment.

Then it went off to Greenland in the terribly cold north. When the ships arrived, they first saw a lot of ice and snow. The knights put on their armor and went ashore to conquer it. But no one was visible and the knights froze in their iron armor on the ice, so they could not move. They kicked wildly, clawing their iron armor hard to free themselves from the ice.

A few of the other soldiers had to make a fire to get them released. As a result, of course, the armor on the feet were pretty hot and the knights burned their feet. They hopped around wildly until they were finally free and quickly disappeared on the ship.

Then one tried to bring the horses ashore, because one should conquer Greenland. The horses struggled hard, but after a few meters they also got stuck in the snow. The soldiers could not walk in the high snow and froze miserably, so that finally all went with their horses back on the ships and Greenland could not conquer first. When the knights sat around thinking and pondering, the lookout on the ship's mast reported "Enemy ahead !!"

And indeed the knights saw in astonishment how a sleigh came with very small horses. They were astonished even more when they discovered that it was not horses but many dogs in front of a sled so effortlessly whizzing across the snow.

Everyone brought their rifles and lances and feared that they would have to defend themselves. But there was only one man on the sled, an Eskimo. He greeted them in a very friendly way and was happy to see so many people, because in Greenland not so many people live and one is often quite lonely and alone. He welcomed everyone and asked them if they would not visit him in the evening, his wife would cook a nice soup of seal meat for them.

From whom you are greeted so friendly, you can fight badly against, and so put three of the knights on the dogsled, but without their heavy armor. Husch - you rushed over the landscape to a strange hut, which was made entirely of snow. It's called an igloo and it's round, but it's very nice and warm!

When they had eaten, they thanked each other and the Eskimo drove them back to their ships by dog sled. Then it was decided to drive back to Denmark.

They then reported everything to the king. He held advice with his ministers how to conquer Greenland. They also asked a wise old man named Count Johannsen. The count whispered his suggestion in the ear of the king and he was thrilled!

He sent his steward to the city to buy whatever vanilla powder he could get. Then he equipped a ship again, but this time the knights should put on thick fur coats and take sledges with them. In addition, the whole load compartment was full of vanilla powder!

Arrived in Greenland, they were greeted by Eskimos again, it was already known by now. The soldiers from Denmark brought a lot of fresh snow and made it with their vanilla powder from delicious vanilla ice cream. They gave it to the Eskimos.

They had never eaten anything like that! They were crazy about it and still wanted to have more. The knights, however, kept everything under wraps and first wanted to speak to the eskimo leader, who was quickly brought for them. With him, the knights made a contract that now Greenland would belong to Denmark and for that the Eskimos would get as much vanilla ice cream as they could eat.

Then the knights sailed home with their ship and told their king that Greenland would now belong to Denmark, without there being a war!

And that's how it is today, so you can ask every Dane.

STORY OF THE LITTLE ANNIKA

I tell you the story of little Annika ...

Annika pulls her blanket up to her chin, presses her teddy tightly to her and pinches her eyes. It does not help anything. She escapes night after night to her parents' safe nest. I can understand Annika very well.

What would you say as a parent so that she is not afraid anymore? Would you try to explain to her that there are no ghosts? Annika would protest. They exist very well! She can hear her. Yes, even feel it.

Annika's mother has an idea.

She places a small, green-shining moon in the nursery and tells her daughter, "Did you know that ghosts are afraid of green light?" Annika looks at her mother with wide eyes. "Ghosts are afraid too?" She asks. "Yes, and they can not harm you when the green moon shines for you."

Annika nods and understands.

Every time Annika hears another giggle or flashes and storms outside, she looks at the moon. She believes in him. Imagines that his green light envelops her. Trust in the wisdom and love of her mother and close her eyes calmly.

Ghosts that adults fear

However, the story continues ...

Annika is growing up. At some point, she no longer needs the green light. The idea of witches and monsters is now funny.

However ... completely different spirits appear in Annika's life.

The worry of not finding the right one. The concern that the money for the rent increase is not enough. The fear that she will never fit in her favorite jeans again ...

Do you think these ghosts are familiar?

Even thirty years later, she can not sleep again because of ghosts. She turns back to her mother.

"You know mom, I sometimes wallow in bed for hours. The worries just do not want to go away. "

"My little one, can you still remember the green moon that drove away all your spirits?"

"Yes. What do you mean by that? A plastic light will hardly be the solution to my worries . These are real! "

Since the mother must first laugh heartily.

"Worries are like ghosts. If you do not believe in them, they can not hurt you. Because worries or fears have only one power: they keep you from concentrating on what you want.

Your attention is like the headlight of a lighthouse. If he rests on what you want, he can not be with your worries. "

The mother chuckles happily and wants to get up. Everything is said for her.

You can not fight worries

"But mom, if I do not solve my worries, then stay! I have to think about her. "

"Have we been dealing with your spirits before? Has your closet broken down, trimmed the feet of your crib or called the Ghostbuster?

No, we did not fight your spirits because they do not exist. Only your attention has given them life. Likewise, your worries only exist in your head. If you try to solve or fight them, they stay alive. "

Annika reflects on her mother's words. If a stranger had told her that, she would have labeled him a reality refugee. However, she has watched her mother too many times, keeping her smile in any challenge. She never had the feeling that she was covering something.

Only now, after she herself knows the wrong ways and ups and downs of life, she appreciates this even more on her mother.

"OK," Annika says. "I'll give it a try. But I no longer believe in the protection of the green moon. I'm sorry."

The mother answers. "You have something much, much better. It's your wishes and dreams. Focus your spotlight on the places you see, the people you laugh with and the successes you want to celebrate.

I promise you that these pictures will come alive every day. "

We are faced with choices countless times every day, either directing our attention to our concerns or to our dreams.

Our life will be guided by this decision.

THE LITTLE FIELD MOUSE CHECKS EVERYTHING EXACTLY

It was a lovely, balmy summer day. The little field mouse and her friends played the whole day in the field by the pond. They played catching, hiding and ran to the bet.

Suddenly the friends laughed. The field mouse had said, "Hello. I'm examining commissioner Stefano Al Dente. I check everything. What should I check? "For fun, the hedgehog had pointed to the blackberry bush and asked:" Can you already eat them? "The little field mouse went to the bush and touched the branches. Then the few blackberries. "Uh-huh. Hm-hm. "She murmured and kept checking. She measured the height of the bush: "Higher than I am tall." And she counted the berries on a branch: "Eleven. More than I am old. "And she took one in her mouth:" Hmmm yum! But not as sweet as I am. "" And? What do you say as a testing expert? "Urged the pig.

"This blackberry bush is awesome. If you want to nibble: go ahead. "And the friends put a few blackberries in their mouths. Then the pig asked, "Check out my football. Should I wish for a new one? "The little field mouse took the football in the paws. She squeezed it and turned it. Then she balanced him on the head. "Ooooh!" Marveled the friends, but the field mouse was not deterred.

She shot the ball against the wall and threw it upright to catch it again. Then she came to a conclusion: "This football is fully in order." "Och manno." The pig got annoyed. "Aaaaber," the field mouse went on, "The abrasion on the surface is immense. Especially good to feel at this point. "She showed the site to friends, but no one could see or feel anything. "I recommend: a new football is urgently needed!" "Yeah!" Rejoiced the pig and shot the football along the dirt road.

"Now me. Now me. "Cried the frog. The field mouse narrowed his eyes and looked at the frog. Then she took a frog's arm in her paws and squeezed and pulled. "Ouch! You know that I'm on it, right? "The field mouse hissed:" Please, absolute rest! I concentrate. "And she looked at the frog from top to bottom. She discovered a birthmark on her left thigh. "What do you have there?" "Well, a birthmark. You can see that, right? "The field mouse shook his head and muttered," Well, well. Like this. Oh dear. "

The frog looked slightly uncertain. Did not something agree with him? Then the field mouse was done with testing and pulled out a note and a pen. She wrote something on it and folded the note and gave it to the frog. He looked quite contrite now. Something was wrong with him. And because of the confidentiality, the field mouse had written it down so that the others would not know. Oh God, oh God.

He took the note and read the text: "Dear frog, you have the all-in-order syndrome. Please DO NOT treat! "

The frog punched the field mouse in the shoulder and said, "All-in-order syndrome? You're crazy! "And they had to laugh.

Brotherchen took his sister by the hand and said: "Since the mother is dead, we have not got an hour left. The stepmother beats us every day, and when we come to her, she pushes us away with her feet. The hard crusts of bread that are left are our food, and the little dog under the table is better off, but sometimes she eats a good bite. That God have mercy! If only our mother knew! Come on, we want to go out into the wide world! "They walked all day through meadows, fields and stones, and when it rained, said the little sister:" God and our hearts, they cry together! "In the evening they came in a big Forest and were so tired of misery, hunger and the long road that they sat down in a hollow tree and fell asleep.

The next morning, when they woke up, the sun was already high in the sky and seemed hot into the tree. Then the little brother said:

"Little sister, I am thirsty, if I knew a little girl, I went and drink once; I mean, I hear one rushing. "Brotherchen got up, took little sister by the hand, and they wanted to look for the Brünnlein. The wicked stepmother, however, was a witch, and she must have seen how the two children had gone away, followed them, secretly, as the witches sneak, and had cursed all the fountains in the forest. When they found a little boy who jumped so glittering over the stones, the brother wanted to drink from it. But the little sister heard, as it said in the murmur: "Whoever drinks from me becomes a tiger, whoever drinks from me becomes a tiger." - Then the little sister called out: "I beg you, little brother, do not drink, otherwise you will a wild animal and tearing me! "The little brother did not drink, whether he was so thirsty, and said:" I want to wait until the next spring. "When they came to the second little brunch, the little sister heard, as this also spoke "Whoever drinks from me becomes a wolf, whoever drinks from me becomes a wolf." Then the little sister exclaimed: "Brother, I beg you, do not drink, otherwise you will become a wolf and eat me!" - The little brother drank not and said, "I want to wait until we come to the next spring, but then I have to drink, you may say what you want, my thirst is too big." And when they came to the third little brunch, the little sister heard as it said in the murmur, "Whoever drinks from me becomes a deer; whoever drinks from me becomes a deer. "The little sister said:" Oh little brother, I beg you, do not drink, or you will become a deer and run away from me. "But the little brother had kneeled down at the little brunch and bent down from him Water drunk and as the first drops had come to his lips, it was there as a Rehkälbchen.

Now the little sister was crying over the poor, cursed little brother, and the rechening also cried and sat beside him so sadly. Then the girl finally spoke: "Shut up, dear little deer, I will never leave you." Then she untied his golden garter, put it around the neck of the buckskin and plucked rushes and braided a soft rope out of it. Then the little creature tied it and carried it on and went deeper and deeper into the forest. And when they had gone long, long, they finally came to a small house, and the girl looked in and because it was empty, thought: Here we can stay and live. The reindeer sought leaves and moss for a soft camp, and every morning it went out and collected roots, berries and nuts, and for the rechen it brought with it tender grass, which it fed from his hand, was cheerful and played in front of him. In the evenings, when Sister was tired and had said his prayer, he put his head on the back of the little Rehkälbchen, that was his pillow, then it fell asleep gently. And if the little brother had only had his human form, it would have been a wonderful life.

It took a while for them to be so alone in the wilderness. It turned out, however, that the king of the country held a great hunt in the forest. The sound of the horns, the barking of the dogs, and the funny yelling of the hunters sounded through the trees, and the deer heard it and would gladly have been there. "Oh," said the little sister, "let me go out into the hunt, I can not stand it any longer!" And asked until it agreed. "But," said it to him, "come back to me in the evening, I shut my door in front of the wild hunters; And so that I may know you, knock and say, 'My little sister, let me in!' And if you do not speak like that, I will not unlock my door. "Now the reindeer jumped out, and he was so well and so funny in the open air. The king and his hunters saw the beautiful animal and put it after him, but they could not catch it and if they thought they had it, it would jump over the bushes and disappear. When it was dark, he ran to the little house, knocked, and said: "My little sister, let me in!" Then the little door was opened for him, it jumped in and rested all night on his soft bed. The next morning the hunt started again, and when the maiden heard the hoisting horn and the "Ho, Ho!" The huntsman, there was no rest and said, "Sister, open me, I have to go out." The little sister opened the door for him and said: "But in the evening you must be there again and say your sayings." When the king and his hunters saw the goddess with the golden collar again, they all chased him, but it was too fast for them nimbly. That lasted all day, but at last the hunters had surrounded it in the evening, and one wounded it a little on the foot, so that it had to limp and slowly ran away. Then a hunter stole after him to the little house and heard how it cried: "My sister, let me in!" And saw that the door was opened to him and immediately locked again. The hunter kept all this in mind, went to the king and told him what he had seen and heard. Then the king said: "Tomorrow shall be hunted again!"

The sister, however, was shocked when he saw that his baby was wounded. He washed off the blood, put herbs on it and said: "Go to your bed, dear Rehchen, that you will be well again." The wound, however, was so small that the reindeer felt nothing in the morning. And when the hunt for the hunt came out again, it said, "I can not stand it, I have to be there; no one should get me so soon! "The little sister wept and said," Now they will kill you, and I am alone in the forest here, and I am deserted from all over the world. I will not let you out. "-" So I'm dying here of sorrow, "answered the deer," when I hear the Hifthorn, I mean, I have to jump out of my shoes! "The sister could not help but close The door opened with a heavy heart, and the rechen jumped into the forest, sound and happy. When the king saw it, he said to his hunters: "Now chase after him all day long into the night, but that no one harm him!" As soon as the sun had set, the king said to the hunter, "Come now show me the little forest house! "And when he was in front of the door, he knocked and shouted:" Dear sister, let me in! "Then the door opened and the king entered, and there stood a girl, that was so beautiful as he had never seen. The girl was startled when she saw that it was not his deer but a man who had a golden crown on his head. But the king looked at it kindly, shook his hand, and said, "Will you go with me to my castle and my dear wife?" - "Oh, yes," answered the girl, "but the rechening must go along with that, too I do not leave. "The king said:" It shall stay with you, as long as you live, and it should lack nothing at all. "In that it jumped in, then tied it again to the Binsenseil, took it in the hand and went away with him from the forest house.

The king took the beautiful girl on his horse and led it into his castle, where the wedding was celebrated with great splendor, and it was now the queen's wife, and they lived together for a long time happily; the deer was cherished and cared for and jumped around in the castle garden. But the wicked stepmother, for whose sake the children had gone into the world, did not mean otherwise, as little sister had been torn to pieces by the wild beasts in the forest, and little brother shot dead by the hunters as a deer calf. When she heard that they were so happy, and they were well, envy and resentment stirred in her heart and left her no peace, and she had no other thought than how she could still bring the two into misfortune , Her right daughter, who was as ugly as the night and had only one eye, reproached her and said: "To become a queen, I should have been lucky." - "Just be quiet," said the old woman, and spoke her contentedly "When it's time, I want to be at hand." Now, when the time had come and the queen had given birth to a beautiful boy and the king was on the hunt, the old witch assumed the form of the chambermaid, He entered the room where the queen lay, and said to the sick man, "Come, the bath is ready, it will do you good and give you fresh strength. Hurry, before it gets cold! "Her daughter was also by the hand, they carried the weak queen into the bath room and put her in the tub, then they shut the door and ran away. In the bathhouse, however, they had turned on a right hell fire, that the beautiful young queen soon had to suffocate.

When that was done, the old woman took her daughter, put a cap on her, and put her to bed at the queen's place. She also gave her the figure and appearance of the queen; only the lost eye could not reproduce her. But so that the king did not notice, she had to lie down on the side where she had no eye. In the evening, when he came home and heard that a son was born to him, he was happy, and wanted to go to the bed of his dear wife and see what she did. Then the old woman shouted quickly: "Be gentle, let the curtains shut, the queen must not yet see into the light and must rest!" The king went back and did not know that a false queen was in bed.

But when it was midnight, and all was asleep, there saw the nurse, who sat in the nursery beside the cradle, and alone watched, as the door opened and the right queen came in. She took the child from the cradle, put it in her arms and gave him a drink. Then she shook his chop, put it back in and covered it with the duvet. She also forgot the Rehchen not, went to the corner where it was, and stroked his back. Then she silently went out the door again, and the nurse asked the guards the next morning to see if anyone had gone to the castle during the night. But they answered, "No, we did not see anyone."

So she came many nights and never spoke a single word; the nanny always saw her, but she did not dare tell anyone.

When such a time had passed, the queen began to speak at night and said:

"What is my child doing? What is my deer doing?

Now I'll come back twice and never again. "

The nanny did not answer her, but when she disappeared again, she went to the king and told him everything. Said the king, "Oh, God! What's this! I want to watch the next night with the child. "In the evening he went to the nursery, but at midnight the queen reappeared and said:

"What is my child doing? What is my deer doing?

Now I'll come again and never again. "

And then used to the child, as she usually did, before she disappeared. The king did not dare speak to her, but he also woke the following night. She spoke again:

"What is my child doing? What is my deer doing?

Now I'll come this time and never again. "

Then the king could not hold himself back, jumped to her and said: "You can be none other than my dear wife!" Then she answered: "Yes,

42

I am your wife," and at the moment by the grace of God had the life was recovered, was fresh, red and healthy. Then she told the king the crime the evil witch and her daughter had committed against her. The king had both brought before the court, and the verdict was pronounced. The daughter was led into the forest, where they tore the wild animals, but the witch was put into the fire and had to burn miserably. And as she was burned to ashes, the little venison turned to become its human form again; Sisters and brothers, however, lived happily together until their demise.

THE ENCHANTED PRINCESS

Once upon a time there was a poor craftsman who had two sons, a good one called Hans and a bath one named Helmerich. But how that goes in the world, the father loved the bad more than the good.

Now it came to pass that the year was once more more than usual, and the master of pouches was empty. Egg! he thought, one must know how to live. If the customers have come to you so often, it's up to you to polite and try to reach out to them. Said and done. Early in the morning he got out and knocked on some stately door; but as it happens the most handsome gentlemen are not the best payers, nobody wanted to pay the bill. Thus the craftsman came home in the evening, and sat down alone in front of the tavern, for he had neither the heart to chat with the diners nor nor he looking forward to his wife's long face, But he was there in thought, he could not but listen to the conversation. A stranger who had just come from a wicked magician and had to stay in the dungeon. Splendid castle with all its treasures. Heimerich is a bright-headed man, who probably wants to barb the goat, so that's one of them called for him ; what is it, he solves the rehearsals and becomes the husband of the beautiful princess and master of land and people. For so the king, her father, had proclaimed. that the beautiful princess was imprisoned by a wicked sorcerer and must remain in the dungeon all her life. Splendid castle with all its treasures. Heimerich is a bright-headed man, who probably wants to barb the goat, so that's one of them called for him ; what is it, he solves the rehearsals and becomes the husband of the beautiful princess and master of land and people. For so the king, her father, had proclaimed. that the beautiful princess was imprisoned by a wicked sorcerer and must remain in the dungeon all her life. Splendid castle with all its treasures. Heimerich is a bright-headed man, who probably wants to barb the goat, so that's one of them called for him ; what is it, he solves the rehearsals and becomes the husband of the beautiful princess and master of land and people. For so the king, her father, had proclaimed. the wizard had set. Splendid castle with all its treasures. Heimerich is a bright-headed man, who probably wants to barb the goat, so that's one of them called for him ; what is it, he solves the rehearsals and becomes the husband of the beautiful princess and master of land and people. For so the king, her father, had proclaimed. the wizard had set. Splendid castle with all its treasures. Heimerich is a bright-headed man, who probably wants to barb the goat, so that's one of them called for him ; what is it, he solves the rehearsals and becomes the husband of the beautiful princess and master of land and people. For so the king, her father, had proclaimed. who probably wants to barb the goat, so that one of him called; what is it, he solves the rehearsals and becomes the husband of the beautiful princess and master of land and people. For so the king, her father, had proclaimed. who probably wants to barb the goat, so that one of him called; what is it, he solves the rehearsals and becomes the husband of the beautiful princess and master of land and people. For so the king, her father, had proclaimed.

Schleunig he returned home and forgot his debts and customers over the new march, which he hurriedly brought his wife. The next morning he said to Heimerich that he wanted to equip him with horse and weir for the journey, and how fast did he set out on the journey! When he said goodbye, he promised his parents that he would have them brought along with the stupid brother Hans in a six-horse carriage; because he already said he was king. Cocky as he drifted, he let go of his will on everything that came in his way. The birds that sat on the branches and praised the Lord God with singing, as they understood it, he shooed with the whip from the branches, and no beasts came in his way, because he had not left out his prankster. And for the first he met an anthill; he had his horse trampled on it, and the ants, who angrily crept to his horse and to himself, and struck horses and men, slew and crushed them all. Next he came to a clear pond in which twelve ducks swam. Helmerich lured them to the shore and killed their eleven, only the twelfth escaped. Finally he met a beautiful hive; There he made it to the bees, as he made it to the ants. And so his joy was to plague and destroy the innocent creature not for the benefit but out of sheer evil. how he made it to the ants. And so his joy was to plague and destroy the innocent creature not for the benefit but out of sheer evil. how he made it to the ants. And so his joy was to plague and destroy the innocent creature not for the benefit but out of sheer evil.

When Helmerich had now reached the magnificent castle in sinking sun, in which the princess was enchanted, he knocked violently at the closed gate. Everything was quiet; the rider throbbed harder and harder. At last a sliding window opened, and out stood an old maiden with a spider-colored face, who morosely asked what he desired. "I will redeem the princess," cried Helmerich. "

Hurry up, son," said the old woman, "tomorrow is also a day, at nine o'clock I'll wait for you here." With that she closed the counter.

The next morning at nine o'clock, when Helmerich reappeared, the little mother was already waiting for him with a small barrel full of linseed, which she spread out on a beautiful meadow. "Read the grains together," she said to the rider, "I'll be back in an hour, then the work has to be done." But Helmerich thought that was a silly joke, and it was not worth bending over; meanwhile he went for a walk, and when the old woman returned, the barrel was as empty as before. "That's not good," she said. Then she took twelve golden keys out of her pocket and threw them one by one into the deep, dark castle pond. "Get the keys up," she said, "I'll be back in an hour, then the work must be done." Helmerich laughed and did as he had done before. When the old woman returned and this task was not solved, she called twice: "Not good! not good! "But she took him by the hand and led him up the stairs to the great hall of the castle; There were three images of women, all three wrapped in thick veils. "Choose, son," said the old woman, "but make sure you choose. I'll be back in an hour. "

Helmerich was no wiser, since she returned when she went away; but he cried out at random: "I'll vote for you on the right." All three of them threw back the veils; In the middle sat the lovely Princess, on the right and left two hideous dragons, and on the right grabbed the Helmerich in his claws and threw him through the window into the deep abyss.

One year had elapsed since Helmerich moved out to redeem the Princess, and still no six-horse carriage had arrived at the parents'. "Oh!" Said the father, "if only the clumsy Hans had moved out instead of our best boy, then the misfortune would have been less."

"Father," Hans said, "let me go, I'll try it, too." But his father did not want to, because what failed the clever, how did the clumsy end? Since the father failed him horse and weir, Hans made secretly and probably wandered for three days the same way on foot, the brother had ridden at one. But he was not afraid and slept at night on the soft moss under the green branches as gently as under the roof of his parents; the birds of the forest did not shy away from him, but sang him to sleep with their best sages. When he came to the ants, busy to complete their new construction, he did not disturb them, but wanted to help them, and he read off the creatures that crawled up against him, without killing them, even if they did bite. He also lured the ducks to the shore, but to feed her with crumbs; He threw the bees the fresh flowers he had picked on the way. So he came cheerfully to the royal palace and knocked modestly at the counter. Immediately the door opened, and the old woman asked for his request. "If I'm not too small, I'd like to try to save the beautiful Princess," he said.

"Try, son," said the old woman, "but if you do not pass the three rehearsals, it will cost your life."

"Well, mother," said Hans, "tell me what to do."

Now the old woman gave give him the sample of flaxseed. Hans was not lazy to stoop, but already it hit three quarters, and the barrel was

47

not half full. He wanted to despair; but suddenly black ants came more than enough, and in a few minutes no grain was left in the meadow.

When the old woman came, she said, "That's good!" And threw the twelve keys into the pond, which he was supposed to get out in an hour. But Hans did not bring a key from the depths; as deep as he dived, he did not get to the bottom. Desperate, he sat down on the shore; Then the twelve ducks came swimming, each with a golden key in their beak, they threw it into the damp grass.

So this sample was also solved when the old woman returned to lead him into the hall, where the third and heaviest rehearsal of him was waiting. Desperately, Hans looked at the three same veiled figures; who should help him here? Then a swarm of bees flew through the open window, circling the room, humming around the mouth of the three wraps. But from the right and left, they flew back quickly, for the dragons smelled of pitch and brimstone, of which they live; The figure in the middle circled them all and whirred and whispered softly: "The Mittle, the Mittle." For then smelled the smell of their own honey, which the princess loved so much.

So, when the old woman returned after an hour, Hans said quite confidently: "I choose the Mittle." And then the evil dragons went out the window, but the beautiful princess threw off her veil and rejoiced in salvation and her beautiful bridegroom. And Hans sent to the father the princess the fastest messenger, and to his parents a golden chariot with six horses, and they all lived gloriously and in joy, and if they have not died, they still live today.

THE BREMEN TOWN MUSICIANS

A man had a donkey who for many years had been carrying the sacks undiminished to the mill, but whose strength was now coming to an end, so that he became more and more unfit for work. Then the master thought to get him out of the food, but the donkey noticed that there was no good wind, ran away and made his way to Bremen; There, he said, he could become a city musician. When he had gone away for a while, he found a hunting dog lying on the road, japping like a man who had run tired. "Well, what are you doing, Packan?" The donkey asked. "Oh," said the dog, "because I am old and grow weaker every day, even in the hunt can not go away, my lord wanted to kill me, so I took a break; but with what shall I earn my bread? "-" Do you know what? "said the donkey, "I go to Bremen and become a city musician there, go with me and let me accept you in the music too. I play the lute and you hit the timpani. "The dog was satisfied, and they went on. It was not long before a cat sat by the way and made a face like three days of rainy weather. "Well, what got in your way, old beard cleaner?" Said the donkey. "Who can be funny when it comes to you," answered the cat, "because I'm coming to age now, my teeth are dull, and I'd rather sit behind the stove and spit, rather than chase mice, mine Women want to drown; I've gotten away, but now good advice is expensive: where should I go? "-" Go with us to Bremen, you understand the night music, then you can become a city musician. "The cat thought that was good and went with it. Thereupon the three exiles flew past a court, where sat on the gate of the house tap and screamed with all his might. "You are shouting through you," said the donkey. "What are you planning to do?" "Well, I prophesied good weather," said the rooster, 'because it is day for our dear women, where they are the little ones to the little Christ child has washed and she wants to dry; but because there are guests coming to-morrow for

Sunday, the housewife has no mercy and has told the cook that she wanted to eat me soup tomorrow, and I should have my head cut off tonight. Now I scream out of my throat as long as I can. "-" Oh well, you redhead, "said the donkey," prefer to leave with us, we're going to Bremen, you can find something better than death everywhere; You have a good voice,

But they could not reach the city of Bremen in one day and came in the evening in a forest, where they wanted to stay overnight. The donkey and the dog lay under a big tree, the cat and the cock made their way into the branches, but the cock flew to the top, where it was safest for him. Before he fell asleep, he looked around again for all four winds, when he saw him, he saw a spark in the distance, and shouted to his companions, it would not have to be a house, for there seemed to be a light. The donkey said: "So we have to get up and go, because here is the hostel bad." The dog said: "A few bones and a little meat on it would do him well." So they made their way to the area where the light was, and saw it soon shining brighter, and it was getting bigger, until they came before a bright, enlightened robber house. The donkey, as the largest, approached the window and looked in. "What do you see, gray horse?" The rooster asked. "What I see?" Replied the donkey, "a table set with fine food and drink, and robbers sit there and be well." - "That would be something for us," said the rooster. "Yes, yes, alas, we would be there!" Said the donkey. Then the animals consulted, how they would have to start to chase out the robbers and finally found a remedy. The donkey had to stand with his forefeet on the window, jump the dog on the donkey's back, climb the cat on the dog, and finally the cock flew up, and sat down on the cat's head. How this had happened, they started on a sign altogether to make their music: the donkey screamed, the dog barked, the cat meowed and the cock crowed. Then they rushed in through the window into the room, making the windows clink. The robbers sprang up at the terrible shouting, meaning nothing else but a ghost came in, and fled in great fear into the forest. Now the four journeymen sat down at the table, took with them what was left, and ate to their heart's content.

As the four minstrels finished, they turned off the light and looked for a place to sleep, each one of its nature and comfort. The donkey lay down on the manure, the dog behind the door, the cat on the stove with the warm ashes, the cock sat on the cocks, and because they were tired from their long way, they soon fell asleep. When midnight was over and the robbers saw from a distance that there was no more light in the house, and everything seemed calm, the captain said: "We should not have let ourselves go into the fenugreek," and ordered one to go and examine the house. The Abyssant found everything quiet, went into the kitchen, lit a candle, and because he looked at the cat's fiery, fiery eyes for living coals, he held a matchstick to catch fire. But the cat understood no fun, jumped in his face, spat and scratched. Then he was terribly frightened, ran and wanted out the back door, but the dog that lay there sprang up and bit his leg, and as he passed the motel across the yard, the donkey gave him a good blow with his hind foot ; but the rooster, who had been wakened from sleep by the noise, called down from the beam: "Kikeriki!" Then the robber ran back to his captain, as he could, and said, "Ah, in the house sits a hideous one Witch, she touched me and scratched my face with her long fingers. And there's a man in front of the door with a knife, he stabbed me in the leg. And there's a black monster in the yard, it hit me with a wooden club. And up on the roof, there sits the judge, he exclaimed, 'Bring me the rascal!' Then I made that I got away. "From now on, the robbers did not dare further into the house, but the four musicians from Bremen liked it so much that they did not want to come out again.

THE COLD SPIRIT

Each season is determined by different weather makers. You already know the godfather Stormwind and the cloud, the rainy spirit. He always awakes from his afternoon nap just when people forget their umbrella at home. But you've probably never heard of Constantine, the cold spirit.

Konstantin is a lazy fellow. Although he is a weather-maker apprentice, he sleeps all summer long. As soon as the sheep's cold and the icy saints are over, he warps into his warm featherbed castle. Konstantin is not responsible for the cool evenings in summer. Nor is he the Bibber King, who conjures up blue lips for all children when they have been in the bathhouse water too long. Konstantin is the little weatherman who only wakes up when the calendar turns into autumn and winter. Then he peels off his thick duvets and yawns extensively. Konstantin is a real frost bag - but he likes to make others freeze.

When everyone is shivering and trembling, Konstantin is so happy that his heart warms. Then Konstantin, the cold spirit, does not freeze anymore. But all the others are shaking their teeth. You'll need to put on tights, an anorak and a hat again, even if you protest vociferously. But thank goodness Konstantin is a real lazybones. He always crawls under his blankets at the beginning of autumn and refuses to let people freeze. Then the sun comes through and it is a wonderful October day. You can wear knee-highs again during the day and you are happy.

A weathermaker apprentice is expected to do the weather for which he was trained. At some point, Konstantin does so with Gevatter Sturm and Father Frost and makes people shiver that it's a real pleasure. Only the Eskimos and polar bears do not quiver. Therefore,

Konstantin does not stop to teach these people to freeze these days. He is content with those who otherwise exist. It makes life mice shiver and in the Himalayas temperatures drop far below zero. This is so exhausting for Konstantin that he will eventually become very, very tired. That's why in the spring he leaves the field to Mother Sun again.

GOOD NIGHT, WIND

The wind swept through the night streets. He rattled the trashcans' lids. He let the branches of the trees thunder against the windows of the houses. With his powerful gusts he made the foliage rustling. When he drove into the doorway, it whistled softly. The wind was loud and he kept Paulchen awake. Because he could not sleep, he jumped out of bed and ran into the kitchen. "Mom, Mom, I can not sleep," he said excitedly to his mother, "The wind is so loud. He will not let me sleep."

His mother gently took him by the hand and led him back to bed. She sat down beside him on the edge of the bed and listened intently to the wind. "Imagine the wind would sing you a lullaby," she said. "Do you hear the melody?" Paulchen said nothing. He, too, listened to the wind. As the air shot through the crack in the door, a tune whistled. The thunder of the branches at the window was as even as it was the clock. As accompaniment rushed the leaves and the garbage bells rattled softly. When little Paul heard the Song of the Wind, he smiled contentedly and snuggled back into the pillows. Slowly his eyes closed and the wind carried him gently to sleep. "Good night, wind.", He muttered sleepily, before he began to dream. When he met the wind in his dream, he humbly thanked him.

SLEEP WELL LITTLE RAINDROPS

Once upon a time there was a small raindrop. Round and shiny, with a spherical, shimmering belly. Together with his family he lived far, high in the clouds in the sky. From here he could see the whole world: the elephants in Africa, the kangaroos in Australia and many, many colorful fish in the oceans.

Every day the little raindrop discovered new animals, places and countries, because the clouds were moving. They moved from left to right and from top to bottom. Sometimes they were very bright and cuddly, sometimes dark and evil. Then they grumbled and made noise. They shook so many raindrops fell to the ground. Like a sea of a thousand tears. The little raindrop, however, sat firmly and securely on its cloud. Satisfied, he looked down and wished that he could visit Earth at some point. He was curious and wanted to see the whole world.

One day a big storm came up. The sky was black and there was a freezing wind. The clouds blew up and shoved. So much so that the little raindrop could not hold anymore. He fell and fell faster and faster towards the earth. He turned in a circle, danced with other raindrops and cheered with joy. Where would he land? With the elephants? With the colorful fish? Maybe in a completely new place? He closed his eyes and let himself drift.

Until he suddenly stopped turning. He stretched out very slowly, opened his eyes and saw that he had landed on something variegated: a dazzling, rain-soaked leaf hanging from a tree. "Hello," said the little raindrop. "Hello," the sheet whispered back. "Nice that you landed on me. So, where do you come from?". The raindrop pointed upwards and could not even believe how far away the clouds had been. They looked tiny.

DHe was almost a little homesick, but then he realized that it was much nicer and warmer on the leaf. And that his journey had taken him pretty hard. "Can I rest a bit with you?" He asked the paper. "Of course. Stay as long as you want. I like company, "he replied. The little raindrop closed his tired eyes and fell asleep. "Sleep well, little raindrop," the sheet still said quietly, wrapping it carefully so it was safe and secure. Then it fell asleep too.

FROM THE SLEEPING APPLE

Once upon a time there was a beautiful old apple tree in a beautiful garden. He was standing in a small village in Styria whose name we do not reveal. As is customary, the apple tree was in full bloom every year and then produced many wonderfully fragrant apples of the variety "Crown Prince Rudolf".

Even our grandmothers knew this Styrian apple variety. They make many apple pie for their grandchildren out of it. Nothing is a proud ending to a ripe Styrian apple, than to be processed by loving hands into baked apples, apple strudel, jams or other goodies. It was also possible to make apple juice for the children and cider for the adults.

At the time of harvest, when the apples were ripe, the first of them fell off the tree by themselves. Then people knew they had to get ladders and harvest apples. Meanwhile, the children played all sorts of games with the apples. They collected apples that had already fallen to the ground into large baskets. No one noticed that one of the most beautiful apples slept blissfully under the canopy and escaped all eyes. He dreamed wonderful dreams that had nothing to do with apple compote or strudel dough. Some apples do not want to be enjoyed as cider, but watch the snowflakes dance or say good night to the night owl. You may want to travel once. But who asks an apple what he wants to do with his life?

Our red-cheeked apple refused to wake up from his blissful slumber. The tree that loves its fruits protected it with its foliage. It's just that an apple can not stay on the tree forever. Gevatter Herbststurm will make sure of that someday. He zaust the apple tree many a day and plucking it from all leaves. Then it's over with the shelter for our apple dreamer. After all, Ms. Holle had a look in and one morning had the snowflake ballet dance. It was snowing and snowing. Our apple woke up from its slumber and was astonished. Since he was the only one left, our apple dreamer soon froze. So after a while he fell into the soft snow bed. The blackbirds who were out of food thanked him for having been waiting for them.

JULIA AND THE LITTLE DRAGON FERDINAND

Many children would like to have an animal, just like you. But many parents do not allow that. And most of the time they have good reasons. But when I was a little kid, I knew a girl named Julia. She was an only child and had no siblings. Little Julia wanted so much to have a dog as a playmate. But the strict father did not allow it.

Julia was so sad that she did not want to eat anything anymore. She often felt lonely. Dad and Mom worked all day. Julia often had to warm up the prepared lunch or go to grandma before she did her homework. Grandma Emmeli looked at her sad granddaughter and thought, "No, that will not work!". She took the girl by the hand and went with her into the forest. There she told the sad child of the little dragon Ferdinand. As a child, Granny had not been allowed to have a cat or a guinea pig, although she longed for an animal. So she had just invented a dwarf village and a little dragon named Ferdinand. Whenever she felt lonely, she imagined stories in her imagination playing in her dwarf village. The dragon Ferdinand was her best friend. Grandma had many adventures with him. Julia wanted to know from grandma where the little dragon had lived. "Well!" Said Granny and laughed: "Under my blanket. The most secret of all places where my parents could not come. "Julia suddenly knew a solution to her problems.

A year later Julia had a best friend named Anna-Lena. Grandma Emmeli wanted to know what they were playing. "That's absolutely secret!" Said Julia. "But I'll tell you as the only human. We sometimes play with other children, but sometimes we also go into the forest and build a tree hollow out of branches. Sometimes my magic dragon "Trollauge" comes to visit and sometimes Anna-Lenàs wild horse "Dreamwind". Honest granny, a best friend is a lot more exciting than anything else. "Yes, Grandma Emmeli understood only too well. And she also understood that sometimes you have to invent a mythical creature that belongs to you all alone to be happy.

PAUL AND THE DANGEROUS WEATHER WITCH

Paul is a little boy, just as old as you are. He can play for hours in the garden. Paul is happy about a rainbow as well as a curious mole. From computers and TVs he holds nothing, because the garden is much more exciting. Paulchen can harvest late wild strawberries and discover hoarfrost on autumn leaves. Hedgehogs sometimes shuffle through the garden at dusk. They lick up the boiled potatoes with milk, which Paul has secretly put under a bush. Paul watches her from his skylight with the telescope.

But everything was bewitched this summer. It was raining when Paul wanted to go swimming. It was stormy-cold as soon as Paul put on his shorts. When he collected tadpoles from the stream to take them home in a jar, a thunderstorm suddenly came on.

"It's like bewitched this summer!" Scolded Paul's father. So Paul came to the conviction that a dangerous weather witch had to be involved. Of course the adults had other explanations - but that does not matter. Parents can not know everything. A weather witch can be very dangerous if left unattended. That's the same with young children. Both have only bad pranks in their heads. Small children, however, have no lightning, no steady rain and no thunder at hand if they want to annoy others.

After Paul had identified the dangerous weather witch as the cause of his problems, he retired to his nursery. He was thinking about a spell to help. It would be great if the weather witch sends rain only at night and unlearns how to make a thunderstorm. Paul tried the spell "Peppery Rubbish Gigantic Rat Thundercrack Cockroach Lake", but nothing happened. He tried "Bumfiedel Drumbinatus Kakalimba Kink Break Frustoribum", but the new spell did not seem to work. The little boy fell asleep over it. But it was also tedious to keep a dangerous weather witch in check.

The next day was beautiful autumn weather. Maybe one of the spells had worked. Paul moved to the pond with Brother Tobias and Neighbor's daughter Ella to catch tadpoles. Of course he did not tell the two of the weather witch.

PRINCESS PINKA AND HER CASTLE

One day Princess Pinka went for a ride in her blue coach. From the carriage Princess Pinka could see many beautiful things - a blue forest, for example, and many blue trees. Princess Pinka thought it was all very nice, but something was missing. Some time later the carriage stopped and Princess Pinka paused. She stood on a blue hill and looked at the world.

But what was that? In the middle of the blue shimmering mountains there was a small valley with a pretty castle. But this castle had a very strange color. There was a beautiful pink castle with small, pink turrets and a large, pink meadow.

Princess Pinka wanted to have a close look at that. She went back to the carriage and continued on the drive. Princess Pinka was very excited. A pink princess lock she had always dreamed of.

She came closer to the castle - but wait, someone was sitting on a pink bench and looked very sad: a pink little princess. Princess Pinka stopped and got off the carriage. "Why are you looking so sad?" She asked the little pink princess. "Oh," said the little princess, "I can not see all this anymore! Every night I dream of a blue castle and whenever I wake it up, it's gone! "Princess Pinka's eyes widened. "Do you know what?" She said. "I'm exactly the other way around! I live in a blue castle. But every night I dream of a castle like this one! "The little princess stood up and could hardly believe it. The two considered for a moment, then they exchanged their clothes and shoes and made their way to their new home. The little princess lived from now on content in the blue castle. Princess Pinka, however, was happy in her new, pink princess castle.

TIMO'S BIRTHDAY RITUAL

Timo has his birthday. Even his sixth. That means Timo is coming to school this year. He can not wait to be one of the big ones who are already in school. He imagines that just great.

There are birthday rituals in Timo's family.

Timo thinks that this year he will be a schoolboy, but at least he wants everything the way it used to be. So in the morning he is awakened by Mama, Papa and Katharina with a Guglhupf, on which the birthday candles are lit. Timo does not like cream cakes, so for him, Guglhupf, baked by grandma, is available. Everyone sings "How nice that you were born, otherwise we would have missed you a lot ..." Timo beams, sits on the edge of the bed and listens to the serenade. He is pressed by everyone, very, very tightly hugged and downed. Then he blows out the candles. If possible, all at once. That was the morning start of the birthday ritual for Timo.

What is done on that day is allowed to determine the birthday child in Timo's family. Maybe a visit to the Tiergarten, sometimes a trip, as in the previous year, when they went by boat. That was really cool. Timo is still raving about it. In the evening, when grandma and grandfather, aunts, uncles, little cousins and even Felix, the dog come along, there are gifts. Of course, Timo can also decide what to eat. That's the same every year - Schnitzel with potato salad, his favorite dish. Especially Timo likes to sit in the middle like on a throne, and everyone in the family tells him why he loves him so much and is happy that there is Timo. This year he does not like to put on a birthday crown anymore. He says he is just too old at the age of six.

THREE LITTLE ASTRONAUT FRIENDS

Max, Mimi and Moritz are sitting in the garden. It is evening. The sun is setting and the three can already see the first stars.

"Look, he's very bright, the star," cries Max.

"That's the evening star," cries Mimi proudly. "I know that, my dad showed it to me yesterday."

"I'd like to see the star closer," Moritz says softly.

"You need a flying ship for that. That way you can go to the moon or to the stars, "says Mimi.

Moritz wants to know that. "Just like a spaceship you need." Mimi knows that. The three sit and think. Where do you get a spaceship? Suddenly Max thinks of something. His little tree house looks just like the spaceship of the Sandman. You just have to rebuild that a bit. Max, Mimi and Moritz love the idea. They bring to Mama what they need: a blanket, a box, a rope and a bucket. Because, these are all things that you can always need. Mom gives them another roll of cardboard. If you look through it, you can see the stars even better. A telescope calls the mama that.

And the three stargazers get something else: a whole basket of food. Mama says that astronauts always eat in their spaceship and they are allowed to do so today. That is exciting. The three bring the things to the tree house. It goes over a small ladder. They make themselves really cozy inside. The blanket comes to the floor. The cardboard roll comes into the box. In the bucket comes the drink and the rope they just tie around. Better safe than sorry. And then it gets very dark and you can see the stars really well. There are so many! The three little astronaut friends look up devoutly for a long time.

The world is so beautiful.

THE MAGICAL SNOWDRIFTS

Ten-year-old Nina walks around town. She wants to go to the library and buy a book. She sees a new business. "Tailor Schneiderlein" Excited she goes inside. "Hello, Mr. Schneiderlein," she greets the tailor. "Oh this stuff with the kittens is nice" says Nina "Do you know that this stuff is a very magical stuff?" Asks Mr. Schneiderlein. "If you hang around the fabric and close your eyes, you can wish for something and it will come true". "I do not believe that, says Nina and shakes her head, there is no such thing." But the tailor tailor puts the fabric around her and tells her to close her eyes and wish for something.

Nina closes her eyes and thinks. She wants to fly. Yes, if that's right with the stuff, let him do that she can fly. "I wanted something," says Nina and Mr. Schneiderlein takes her cloth cloak away. "Then try if it worked," he says. Nina spreads her arms and swings her up and down and it really works. She flies around in the shop and finally she flies out of the door, high in the sky. How nice it is to be able to fly with the birds around the bet. There she sees a robber of an old woman pulling a necklace from her neck and taking it with her. A street ahead she sees a policeman. She flies down and explains what she has seen. "Girl, do not lie to me, nobody can fly," says the policeman and does not budge.

What now? Nina shows him she can fly. The policeman is astonished and follows her and arrests the robber. The old woman gets her chain back and she thanks her with some money and sweets. What a great day Nina thinks and flies away.

THE SLUMBER PARTY

Lotte is very excited. She is invited to the pajama party with her friend Mia today. "Shall I put on my pajamas right away?" She asks, not waiting for the answer. She gets her favorite pajamas out of bed and begins to change. "Stop, stop!" Laughs her mom, "we'll pack that in your backpack. And the toothbrush also has to go along with it. "" And Carlo, he has to go, too, "says Lotte." He's usually scared when I'm not there. "Carlo is Lotte's favorite cuddly bunny.

Then they set off. Mia, her parents, and her brother Max live in the same street, just three blocks away. The house is already quite funny. Not only Mia is there but also Sarah, Jonas, Aylin, Felix, Carolin and Lena - all from Lotte's kindergarten. Apart from Lotte, all children are actually in nightwear. Lotte thinks that's funny. She has only ever seen Mia in her nightgown when she once stayed with her. Jonas wears a pajamas on with a red racing car and Felix on with dinosaurs. Lotte suddenly thinks, "I hope nobody laughs because I brought Carlo ..." But then she forgot the thought again, as Mia pulls them by the hand, down the stairs into the large living room. They play "Journey to Jerusalem", but not with chairs but with cushions. And some other games that Mia's mom knows. You will not get tired this evening. Mia's mom later reads two bedtime stories.

All at once, Lotte sees Jonas sitting quietly on his pillow on the floor. He looks sad. Lotte has an idea. She gets Carlos out of Mia's room and sits next to Jonas. "That's Carlos," she says quietly, holding it out to Jonas. "Carlos is a scaredy cat. Do you like to protect him? "Jonas nods and grins a bit. Now he does not look as sad as he did before ...

A SMALL SHOP IN AN EVEN SMALLER PLACE

Mr Krämer is standing in front of his shop and beckons Otto cheerfully as he gets out of the school bus. "Hello Mr. Krämer!", Exclaims Otto and runs to meet him.

"Well, how was it at school?" Asks Mr. Krämer. "It went like this.", Mumbles Otto. Since he has to go to the big school in the neighboring village, Otto does not make learning fun anymore. His old school was much smaller and somehow more comfortable. It has been closed since last summer. Also the flower shop and the newsstand are gone. Only Mr. Krämer with his little shop is still there. Otto hopes that it stays that way, because he likes to be with Mr Krämer. The store has a thousand things to discover. It is flashing, sparkling, buzzing and whirring. In addition, Mr. Krämer can tell the most exciting stories.

Today Otto is brave and asks: "Are you going away too?" Mr. Krämer strokes Otto gently over his head and smiles. "Come on." Otto grabs his hand and the two disappear in the back of the shop. Otto has never been here. Now he stands with open mouth in front of countless photos. On each photo you can see the small shop of Mr. Krämer. His little village does not see Otto. He sees high mountains, Africa, penguins in the snow, skyscrapers and deserted islands.

"But?" Otto is speechless. How is that possible? Mr Krämer puts his hand reassuringly on Otto's shoulder. "I am always where I am needed. Now you need me. "

Otto still does not understand. Confused, he sits down on the big, blue sofa. "Would you like a cocoa?" Asks Mr. Krämer. Otto nods. Mr. Krämer points his finger at the table. It is followed by a flash of lightning and before Otto is a steaming cup of cocoa. Now Otto understands and grins over the whole face. Mr. Krämer laughs, too. "But that remains our secret, promised?" Asks Mr. Krämer. "Of course," says Otto, sipping his cocoa.

A BREATHTAKING GONDOLA RIDE

One evening, cuddly animal Balthasar looked out of the window. There he saw a sea of flashing lights moving back and forth. He wanted to know what that was, so he asked his bear sister Abigail. She said that these were gondolas with lights attached. Balthasar had no idea what that meant and continued to tease Abigail with questions.

"What are gondolas and why do they light up?"

Abigail replied: "This is called notch, fair, free market, fair or cathedral. People go there to have fun. They sit in flashing gondolas that turn around themselves or overhead. "

" I want to try that, too, "Balthasar replied, yelling with anticipation.

"But Balthasar, you know we can not go out alone."

"Yesterday, Annabelle said she would like to visit the fair tomorrow at noon. I'm sneaking into her backpack in the morning, so I'm not alone! "

" That's a bad idea. What if she loses her backpack? "

" She will not, I'm in! "

" But Baaaaalllthaaasar, she does not know that! "

"Oops, right. I'll still sneak into my backpack anyway. I do not always just want to be in bed, I also want to experience something. "

Worried, Abigail looked after Balthasar the next morning, already squeezing into Annabelle's backpack. He waited excitedly in the backpack until it was time.

Arrived at the fair Balthasar suddenly felt like something wobbled. He dared and opened a piece of the zipper. He was sitting in a wobbly gondola, which was always higher and could look out over the city.

Once home, he told Abigail about this great event and she explained:

"Balthasar, you went Ferris wheel! Luckily, you did not get dizzy. "

Balthasar obviously seemed to like the ride very much , since he fell asleep when Annabelle had covered him.

THE ENDLESS QUEUE

Once upon a time, two siblings, a boy and a girl, lived on a distant planet. This planet was actually very similar to our planet, but some of them could even do magic. In the midst of all this, one day Janina went shopping with her brother Karl, because her mom wanted to bake a cake. There it does not look quite as you imagine a department store. No, even in the summer it was all over decorated with beautiful things. For example, at the top of the field is a yellow sunflower, just as you know it, and at night the department store shone in bright colors.

Once in the store, they took out their note with the ingredients and loaded them, one by one, into the shopping basket. Soon they were finished and went to one of the numerous coffers. There were a lot of people there, Janina and Karl seemed like an endless queue. They talked softly while the other people paid their purchases. But after a while Karl became a little thoughtful: "You Janina, why are we still in the same place as before?" And indeed, they had not moved forward. During the whole time!

Janina answered, "How can it be that only the others, but not we come to pay?" The two were already a bit sad, as spread a wide grin on the face of Karl: "Sister, me I know it. Mother said we should stomp with our feet if we need a little magic help. And this way: once with the left, and once with the right. "Of course, both tried immediately. And indeed, it worked. Already, suddenly, they were standing in front of the cash register. So they could pay everything from mother's money. Happy, they went home and were looking forward to the cake.

BEAR BRUNO DOES NOT LIKE TO SLEEP

Bruno the bear is always very tired in the evening. Mama Bear then puts him in his cuddly bear bed and covers him lovingly. She reads to little Bruno every night before a bedtime story. Bruno likes the story of the two squirrels who always forget where they have hidden their nuts. But if Mama Bear believes that tired Bruno falls asleep peacefully after the good night story, she was wrong. Bruno the little bear just does not want to fall asleep. He could miss one of the many exciting bedtime stories Mama Bär knows.

"Potzblitz", Mama Bär often thinks, it's not easy to make a small brown bear tired. All day long, little Bruno romps around with his siblings and practices somersaulting in front of the Bear Cave. He climbs small trees and chases butterflies in the grass. Actually, he would have to be very, very tired in the evening. The big siblings, who are already in the bear school, go to bed every night. Immediately fall asleep after Dad's bear's bedtime story, dreaming of fractions and the bear alphabet.

Only little Bruno is still wide awake because he is looking forward to the bedtime stories all day long. Sometimes Mama Bär has to tell him three stories in a row. But if you think that the little rascal then falls asleep, you were wrong. Only Mama Bear snores loudly in her reading-chair, because reading made her tired. How can a little bear cub sleep there?

One day grandma Braunbär came to visit. The old bearded lady was very impressive. She always knew some advice. When Mama Baer told her that little Bruno simply did not want to fall asleep, Grandma Baer just laughed. She said, "I'll tell you a secret that my great-grandmother once entrusted to me. Do not read bedtime stories to your little bear cub, but promise him a good morning story! You'll see what happens then. "

That's exactly what Mama Bear did. Little Bruno was very disappointed. He cried bitterly, but Mama Bear said, "The sooner you fall asleep now, little Bruno, the sooner it will be bright day again and I'll tell you a good morning story at breakfast. Unfortunately, my stock of bedtime stories has been used up. "

When little Bruno woke up the next morning, Mama Baer wanted to keep her promise. Little Bruno jumped out of bed happily. He shouted, "Unfortunately I have no time for stories. I'd rather practice flip-flops with Brummel and see if the sun is shining. "

THE DRAGON AND THE WIND

More momentum! "Arthuro looked down a little anxiously from the top of the mountain. He was a 2-meter-long, blue-green dragon with bright yellow eyes, large silver spines - and today he practiced flying with his dad. But it was a bit more difficult than he thought: what if he fell from the air and broke a wing?

"Arthur, more momentum!" Arthur and his dad were practicing Arthur's new paper kite down the mountain. It just did not work out because the wind did not blow so hard and Arthur had to walk really fast, so the kite came up a bit. And unfortunately he never stayed up for more than a few seconds ...

"Come, I'll show you again!" Arthuro's dad flew on the spot. It worked! Arthuro was excited, but the October wind up here was just right for him, and he wore it fantastically.

"Great, Arthur! Just a little more! "The brown-haired boy with the freckles on his nose ran faster than ever. Nevertheless, he wished for a bit more wind. Then it would be even easier. When he looked up at the mountain for a moment, he did not believe his eyes: "Daddy - look! A little dragon is practicing with his daddy! "" Only the flag at the summit cross broke loose ", his dad laughed" Go on, run another round. "

Arthuro was flying so safely and happily now that he had almost made it halfway up the mountain. When he saw the boy with the paper kite, he landed behind a pile of stones and watched him curiously. Just that second, the human boy told his dad how nice it would be if his paper kite could fly as well as the little dragon on the mountain. "Yes, yes, my noble knight! Dragons are special animals! And you really have a lot of feeling for her, be it real or paper. "

The little dragon was very happy about the praise and decided to take the boy under the wings. How good that he could not spit fire! He took a deep breath and blew through his nostrils as hard as he could. "Hooray, he's flying!" Arthur was pleased because his paper kite not only stayed in the air, but played well with the wind - depending on how much air Arthuro blew out of his hiding place. "Have fun, little man," he thought. "Maybe we can play together once! After all, you're good and careful with dragons! "

MOM, WHO IS MAKING THE WIND?

Lisa goes with her mom to the kindergarten. Lisa is a girl with two little pigtails that hang over her ears day after day. She is also a very funny girl who likes to know everything and therefore often asks many questions. Sometimes there are so many questions, sometimes she finds the answers very difficult. Then she has to come up with an answer herself.

It is a gray morning. "Gray can be different," says Lisa. The adults do not like the gray sky in the fall, they find it boring. Lisa likes to watch gray clouds. She sometimes walks with her head up, keeping her face in the direction of the gray clouds passing by in the sky. She thinks that some clouds look like cuddly animals. Mama always has to laugh about Lisa. But Lisa may just go with her head in the clouds.

,This morning it is especially exciting. The clouds are running a race today. Lisa is watching a small, bright cloud sheep take a lead in front of a large, dark cloud animal. Lisa claps her hands with joy. Mama says: "This is the wind that makes the clouds run so fast in the sky". Lisa stops. She did not think about that. She must immediately think of the fun game they have been doing in kindergarten for a few days. Lisa and other children stand in a circle, holding up their arms, wiggling, blowing with all their might. They have learned that wind moves tree branches.

Then her mum shows a series of brown autumn leaves that magically rise from the ground and spin in the air. "The wind also makes the leaves dance," says Mama. Lisa looks deeply into her mum's face and must quickly ask a question: "Mom, who's doing the wind?"

Again, this is a question to which Mama finds only one difficult answer: "Wind is air that flees from one place to another. She is in a hurry. "Lisa wants to know more precisely:" But who makes the wind?

78

"Mom tries again:" When the air gets warm from the sun, it becomes light and rises. Then cold air comes down, until it gets warm too. So the warm and the cold air volumes always exchange their places. "Before Lisa can ask the next question, Mama finds that they have to hurry to get to kindergarten on time. Lisa moans, then she has to come up with an answer herself.

When they finally arrived in the warm kindergarten, Lisa was suddenly all right. Of course! The air is in a hurry to arrive in a warm place. Lisa could understand that very well.

CINDERELLA FAIRYTALE STORY

Once upon a time there was a girl named Cinderella who lived with her stepmother and two stepsisters. Poor Cinderella had to work hard the whole day so the rest could rest. She had to wake up every morning when it was dark and cold to light the fire. She cooked the meals. It was she who kept the fire running. The poor girl could not stay clean of the ashes and ashes by the fire.

"What a mess!" Laughed her two step-sisters. That's why they called her "Cinderella."

One day big news came to the city. The king and queen would have a ball! It was time the prince found a bride. All the young ladies in the country were invited to come. They were wild with joy! They would put on their most beautiful dress and dress their hair beautifully. Maybe the prince would like her!

With Cinderella, she now had extra work to do. She had to make two brand new dresses for her step-sisters.

"Faster!" Cried a stepsister.

"You call that a dress?" The other shouted.

"Oh dear!" Cinderella said. "When can I-"

The stepmother marched into the room. "When can you WHAT?"

"Well," said the girl, "when will I have time to make my own dress for the ball?"

"You?" Cried the stepmother. "Who said YOU would go to the ball?"

"What a laugh!" Said a stepsister.

"Such a chaos!" They pointed to Cinderella. Everyone laughed.

Cinderella said to herself, "If you look at me, you may see a mess. But I am not like that. And if I could, I would go to the ball. "

Soon it was time for the stepmother and step-sisters to go to the big party. Her beautiful carriage came to the door. The stepmother and step-sisters hopped in. And they were gone.

"Goodbye!" Cried Cinderella. "Have fun!" But her stepmother and step-sisters did not turn around to see her.

"Ah, me!" Cinderella said sadly. The carriage drove down the street. She said aloud, "I wish I could go to the ball, too!"

Then - Phew!

Suddenly, a fairy was in front of her.

"I wish I could go to the ball, too!"

"You have called?" Said the fairy.

"I have?" Cinderella said. "Who are you?"

"Well, of course, your fairy goddess! I know your wish And I have come to grant it."

"But ..." said Cinderella, "my wish is impossible."

"Excuse me!" Said the fairy godmother angrily. "Did not I just pop out of nowhere?"

"Yes, you have," said Cinderella.

"Then let me be the one who says what is possible or not!"

"Well, I think you know that I also want to go to the ball." She looked at her dirty clothes. "But look at me."

"You look a bit confused, kic," the fairy godmother said.

"Even if I had something beautiful to wear," the girl said, "I would not have a way there."

"Love me, all this is possible," said the fairy. She tapped her wand on Cinderella's head.

Cinderella was suddenly clean. She wore a beautiful blue dress. Her hair was set high in her head in a golden ribbon.

"That's wonderful!" Said Cinderella.

"Who said I'm done?" Said the fairy godmother. She tapped her wand again. Immediately afterwards, a beautiful carriage with a driver and four white horses was born.

"Do I dream?" Cinderella said, looking around.

"It's as real as it can be real," said the fairy godmother. "But there is one thing you need to know."

"What's this?"

"All this only lasts until midnight. Tonight, at midnight, it's all over. Everything will be as it was before. "

"Then I have to be sure to leave the ball before midnight!" Cinderella said.

"Good idea," said the fairy godmother. She stepped back. "My work is done." And with that the fairy godmother was gone.

"It only lasts until midnight."

Cinderella looked around. "Did that happen?" But there she stood in a beautiful dress and had a golden band in her hair. Before her waited her driver and four horses.

"Comes?" Called the driver.

She got into the carriage. And they were gone.

On the ball, the prince did not know what to think. "Why do you have that sad expression on your face?" The queen said to her son. "Look around, you could not ask for more beautiful girls than these."

"I know, mother," said the prince. Still, he knew something was wrong. He had met many of the young women. However, after saying "hello" bit by bit, he could not say anything anymore.

"Appearance!" Someone pointed to the front door. "Who is this?"

All heads turned around. Who was the beautiful girl who went down the stairs? She held her head tall and looked as if she belonged to it.

But nobody knew her.

"There's something about her," the prince said to himself. "I will ask her to dance." And he went over to Cinderella.

"We've met?" Said the prince.

"I am pleased to meet you now," Cinderella said with a bow.

"I feel as if I know you," the prince said. "But of course that's impossible."

"Many things are possible," Cinderella said, "if you want them to be true."

The prince felt a leap in his heart. He and Cinderella danced. When the song was over, they danced again. And then they danced again and again. Soon, the other virgins on the ball were jealous. "Why is he dancing with her all the time?" They said. "How rude!"

But the prince could only see Cinderella. They laughed and talked and danced even more. In fact, they danced so long that Cinderella did not see the clock.

"Dong!" Said the clock.

Cinderella looked up.

"Dong!" Went the clock again.

She looked up again. "Oh, my!", She exclaimed. "It's almost midnight!"

"Dong!" The watch rang.

"Why is that important?" Said the prince.

"Dong!" Cried the clock.

"I have to go!" Cinderella said.

"Dong!" Went the clock.

"Oh my!" She screamed. "It's almost midnight!"

"But we just met!" Said the prince. "Why go now?"

"Dong!" The watch rang.

"I have to go!" Cinderella said. She ran to the stairs.

ran on.

"Dong!" Said the clock.

"Please wait a moment!" Said the prince.

"Dong!" The watch rang.

"Goodbye!" Cinderella turned around one last time. Then she stormed out of the door.

"Dong!" The clock was quiet. It was midnight.

"Wait!" Cried the prince. He lifted her glass slipper and stormed out the door. He looked around but could not see her blue dress anywhere. "That's all I have left of hers," he said, looking down at the glass slipper. He saw that it was done in a special way to fit a foot like no other. "There's another glass slipper somewhere," he said. "And if I find it, I will find it too. Then I will bite her to be my bride! "

From hut to hut, from house to house, the prince went. A young woman to the other try to put her foot in the glass shoe. But nobody could match. And the prince moved on.

Finally the prince came to Cinderella's house.

"He's coming!" Cried a stepsister and looked out the window.

"At the door!" Shouted the other stepsister.

"Quick!" Cried the stepmother. "Get ready, one of you has to be the one to fit your foot into this slipper, no matter what!"

The prince knocked. The stepmother opened the door. "Come in!" She said. "I have two beautiful daughters you can see."

The first stepsister tried to put her foot in the glass shoe. They try hard, but it just would not work. Then the second stepsister tried to put her foot inside. They tried it with all their strength. But no dice.

"Are there no other young women in the house?" Said the prince.

"None," said the stepmother.

"Then I have to go," said the prince.

"Maybe there is one more," Cinderella said, stepping into the room.

"I thought you said there were no other young women here," the prince said.

"Nothing of importance!" Said the stepmother hissing.

"Come here," said the prince

Cinderella came up to him. The prince dropped to one knee and tried the glass shoe on her foot. It fits perfectly! Then Cinderella took something out of her bag. It was the other glass slipper!

"I knew it!" He exclaimed. "You are the one!"

"WAR?" Called a stepsister.

"Not YOU!" Shouted the other stepsister.

"That can not be!" Cried the stepmother.

But it was too late. The prince knew that Cinderella was the one. He looked into her eyes. He saw neither the ashes in her hair nor the ashes in her face.

"I found you!" He said.

"And I found you," Cinderella said.

And so Cinderella and the Prince were married and lived happily ever after.

FALL COMES

Anna, the bat cheekily stretched her nose out of the barn and blinked out. Yes, she could smell it very clearly, it was in the air. Trial, yes - clearly, the air smelled of autumn, after plowed, fresh earth. Her dwelling, the barn, belonged to Peter's father. Peter and his parents lived on this farm. The large barn served as a shelter for Anna and her bat friends. A good place to sleep!

Peter met Anna, the bat, in front of the barn and said mysteriously: "Anna, the time has come! It's autumn and my party is tomorrow! Are you ready for the show again and inform your friends? "The bat fluttered excitedly around the trees! On to the other bats, because they too should know: It started again!

Peter was already cutting out pumpkin heads and decorating the courtyard with it, tealights made their faces shine. Artificial cobwebs were draped on fences and walls and blankets turned into ghosts. It was supposed to be a bit mysterious. The guests came and it was wildly celebrated and raged. Everyone was dressed as ghosts, witches or vampires and now the show would start!

The disguised started in the corn field. Peter's father had built a corn maze out of it and the children were already looking for the exit. In the half-dark, the children ran around laughing to find the right path.

Peter gave the signal: he whistles!

And already the bats started their flight! They whizzed wildly across the cornfield and with dives the bats flew just above the heads of the children until they shrieked and laughed. "The bats are doing their show with us - juchuuu!" The children shouted.
Again and again the bats fluttered around the children and everyone had a lot of fun! Anna laughed and Peter called her as the bat tie pulled off towards the barn: "Anna again next year!

87

NOW IT IS CYCLED

When Papa Bär came home from work, he said cheerfully to Mama Bär and son Tommy: "Today is a beautiful summer evening! We're going on an excursion: Now it's time to cycle! "Mama Bär packed a few treats and drinks and the bear family stowed everything in their bicycle baskets. Tommy Bär was really happy - a picnic bike ride would be fun! The three started happily and their way led them past meadows, brooks, lakes and through forests and their bicycles rolled through their lively kicks on the pedals ever further through the beautiful nature.

Tommy Bär exclaimed excitedly, "Mom, daddy, we'll pass Patty Hase's house right away - may she drive with us?" Mama and Papa Bear had nothing against it and so Tommy knocked on the door of the hare. After Patty had received permission from Mama and Papa Hase, the group now cycled on to four, ready to find a picnic spot soon and dine with relish.

During a forest clearing, the three bears and Patty Hase found a place that was wonderful for the picnic. A large tree provided shade and the clearing opened up a small patch of meadow. There Tommy and Patty could play after strengthening a little ball, because Patty had well-given a ball in her basket. Oh, how funny that would be!

After they ate on the picnic blanket all sorts of delicacies such as honey, carrots, apples, ham, cheese and some honey biscuits and drank milk and cocoa, they went to the meadow. The ball flew back and forth and the little bear and the bunny girl played the cheerful throwing and catching game. From time to time Mama and Papa Bär were also present and they played with the ball by four.

Now they had to make their way back slowly, because soon the sun would set. Strengthened by the picnic and happy in their hearts, they delivered Patty to the rabbit and drove home.

THE BLUE KINGFISHER

Eight-year-old Jessica lived with her parents near a footpath. This snaked along a branch of the river. On Sundays people drove on it with the rowboat for a walk. They enjoyed the weeping willows and giant trees that dipped low over the river.

It was shady on the riverbank, quiet and mysterious. Jessica was not allowed to go near the shore alone - but sometimes she did. There was a blue bench standing on a small peninsula on the riverbank. She sometimes went there on Sunday mornings to watch Canada geese. The girl just sat there, watching those wonderful birds gather in droves and hear their loud chatter. Jessica thought this was a place full of magic. She was all alone with the geese. Jessica imagined that piece of forest by the river was hers alone. But of course we humans are only guests in nature. It belongs to itself. And it is full of miracles.

One morning, while the parents were still asleep, Jessica was sitting on her bench by the river again, waiting for the geese. But they did not come that morning. Instead, a small blue kingfisher came. He sat down on one of the branches on the edge of the water. Jessica hardly dared to breathe, so pretty was the little bird with its orange-yellow tummy and the bright blue plumage. She had never seen such a beautiful bird before. Suddenly the little kingfisher shot into the water. He soon reappeared with a small fish in his beak. Jessica behaved as quiet as a mouse. The bright blue bird flew back to the branch he had been sitting on and ate his fish. After that, he sat quietly on his branch for a while. He seemed to sleep. Suddenly a branch cracked somewhere and the shy bird flew away.

Jessica quickly walked home to tell her parents about this wonderful experience. Of course, the two scolded, because they were already worried. Little girls are not allowed to go to a river alone. But that Jessica loved nature so much, the parents could understand well.

THE TICKLISH CANOE

Far away in America, there lives the little Indian Pintu with his parents in a colorful Indian tent.

Today is Pintu's birthday. "You are already a big boy. That's why you get your own canoe, "says Pintu's father.

Pintu is very happy. He was allowed to ride with the adults, and even row. But the adults' canoes were far too big for him and hard to steer.

His own canoe is just right. It is smaller than an adult canoe and much more colorful and fun painted.

Pintu grabs his new canoe and runs down to the river. Pintu's mother is worried. "What if the river's current is too strong and the waves are too high?" "Do not worry, it's a very special canoe, nothing can happen to it!" Laughs Pintu's father.

Down the river, Pintu wants to let the canoe into the water. The river is very restless and wild at this point, but Pintu feels brave.

As he lets the canoe into the water, it suddenly starts to jump and giggle, so Pintu can not get in. "What's going on?" Asks Pintu. "I'm so ticklish, I can not be in the water with strong currents and high waves. Get me out! "Says the canoe. Pintu wonders. A canoe that can speak and is ticklish? What should he do with a ticklish canoe? "Let me into the water in a quiet place." Suggest the canoe. "The currents and waves do not tickle me and it's safer for you." Pintu likes the idea. He takes the canoe and leaves it in a quiet place in the water. Here the canoe does not jump and chuckle. Pintu can get in and both paddle happily on the river. If the water wilder, the small canoe does not continue, because it is far too ticklish.

Pintu's parents do not have to worry about Pintu being in danger.

THE MAGIC BOOK

Outside, a terrible storm was raging. Sonja lay bored on the bed. She leafed through a storybook. It was a birthday present from her aunt. After a while she fell asleep slowly. When she woke up, Sonja found herself on a lush green field. Confused, she stood up. How had she come here? Feverishly she thought about what to do now. Since she was a stranger to the area, she just ran in one direction. At first, Sonja saw nothing except many tall trees and shrubs.

The girl did not want to be beaten. She was a brave child after all. She would simply seek help. Somebody had to be here somewhere.

She continued for a while and finally came to a small house. White steam rose from the chimney. The enticing scent of cinnamon buns spilled out of the cracks in the window.

Tentatively, Sonja knocked on the door. Almost immediately, this was opened. An old woman with snow-white hair and very red cheeks behind. "Hello," Sonja said uncertainly. I was probably lost. Can you tell me how to find my way back to my room? - "Come in first," the woman replied cheerfully. "Have no fear. Here, try my fresh cinnamon rolls. It's just finished. "

Sonja sat down nicely at the table and bit into the pastry. It tasted heavenly. The dough was silky soft. The vanilla sugar melted on the tongue and the raisins made it very juicy. She was served warm cocoa. She ate until she was full. Then her eyes closed again.

The next time she woke up, she was surprisingly on bed again. Sonja realized that she had probably dreamed. She was about to slam the book when the old woman from the dream winked at her from one side.

MRS. HEXHEX

Every day on the way to school and back again Olivia runs past a beautiful house where an old lady lives. Sometimes she sees her in the front yard, but she never says anything to her. The other children say that the old woman is a bad witch. One day, Olivia forgets her schoolbag in the school bus. But she not realizes it until she is almost in front of the old woman's house. "Oh no, shit!" Says Olivia when she realizes it. As always, the old lady is standing in her front yard. "What is it, my child?" She asks softly. Olivia answers politely what happened. "Maybe your dad can pick up the satchel at the nearest bus stop?"

But Olivia does not dare to tell her parents that she was so fussy and forgot her bag. "Hm," says the old woman. "Maybe I can help". "She? But you're a wicked witch ... "Olivia quickly puts her hand over her mouth. "I'm sorry, the other kids say that". The old woman just smiles. "I am the woman Hexhex. And you, what is your name? "" I am Olivia. You are not angry? "The old lady now giggles" No. Come in the front yard ". Olivia goes to her.

Mrs. Hexhex mumbles something and suddenly a broom comes flying. "Come on, get up," she says, helping Olivia climb the broom. The broom rises in the air and both fly high up. Olivia is excited "Mrs. Hexhex, where are we flying?". "Let yourself be surprised," she says and pushes the tube. Hui, that was a wind! After a few minutes they arrive at the next bus stop and land next to the bus. Olivia can bring her schoolbag and is happy. "Ms. Hexhex, you are a good witch and have helped me so much," she calls, back up in the air and shining all over her face.

THE PIRATE CAKE

Lotta wants to be just one thing in her life: a real pirate. That must be an exciting life. Every day adventure, every day doing what you want. Well, not quite. Of course, Lotta knows that as a pirate you have to obey his captain. That does not matter, of course Lotta wants to be captain. "Pirate captain Lotta," that sounds great.

Lotta has her birthday soon. She is five years old. She is already very excited, birthday is something nice. You get visitors, you get presents and you get a really great cake. Wait - Lotta is a bit scared. Eating pirate pies? Lotta has never heard that, real pirates eat fish fingers and stuff like that. But cake? Lotta thinks for a long time. She wants so much to be a pirate, but she also wants a really great birthday cake.

In the evening, Lotta asks the dad if pirates eat cake. But sure, the dad says, pirates are constantly eating pie. Every Sunday and every birthday. But not some cake, it must be a real pirate cake. And for that you need a secret recipe. A very real, secret pirate pie recipe.

The next day, the dad comes with a note that looks like a treasure map. Lotta has already seen treasure maps in her pirate book. She knows her stuff. It's not a treasure map, it's a real recipe for a pirate cake. Dad bought it from an old pirate he met in a bookstore. Did Daddy say.

The next day, Dad and Lotta bake the pirate cake all by themselves. And that will be great. It becomes a very fine cake, with nuts and chocolate in it. And it is decorated: Papa and Lotta color the cake blue and make a pirate ship made of marzipan. The ship put her on the cake on top of it. Because there is still a bit of marzipan left, they knead some fish. Then the pirate cake is ready. It is the most beautiful pirate cake in the world!

THE FIREFLY TREE

Anna was already sitting at supper when Valentin came in. Valentin asked: "Anna, are you coming? My cat Minka is gone and I have to find her again before it gets dark! "Anna immediately jumped up and joined her boyfriend. She slipped into her warm jacket and set off with Valentin. The day had been beautiful and Anna had played with Valentin and his cat until Mama called for supper.

"Minka come, come on, little kitten!" The children called with curiosity for the red-brown tabby. They searched the house, the garden and the stable. Suddenly Anna called excitedly: "Valentin, look, here I can see a cat track!" Valentin came quickly. He was very excited. "Yes, I see her too. Come on, we'll run after you! "The two friends took each other by the hand. Valentin looked again more closely at the track. "Did you see Anna? There's a firefly sitting there. We have to hurry, because soon the night will come! "Anna looked forward to the front. The children realized that it was already starting to get dark. "Look, Valentin, there is still a firefly sitting there!" Anna answered. The children ran together to the little animal.

Even before the cute beetle's bulb went out, Anna and Valentin spotted another trace of the little cat. The children were surprised only briefly and then continued to search. Anna squeezed Valentine's hand tight and pulled him forward. "Valentin, Valentin, here are even more fireflies. I think they show us the way! "Anna and Valentin followed the glowing trail and came to a tree that was covered with fireflies all over.

Minka sat with glowing eyes on a branch and moaned miserably. But the tree chosen by the little cat was full of fireflies and seemed as bright as the sun. Valentine climbed nimbly on the tree and happily brought down his little kitten again. Even before it got really dark, the friends made their way home and gave their milk to the little runaway. Silently, Anna said before she moved away from the tree, "Thank you, little fireflies, you showed us the way!"

BEDTIME STORIES FOR KIDS

Meditation Stories to Help Children Fall Asleep Fast and Feel Calm, Learn Mindfulness and Reduce Anxiety. Beautiful Self-Healing Tales for Mind, Body and Soul

BY

Kelly Joyful

THE TWO MEADOW MICE

Once upon a time, two mice lived on a meadow. One was very busy. From morning to night she collected supplies for the winter. She dug up roots, carried the seeds of grasses into her cave, fetched tubers and fruits, filling one storehouse cave after another. Worried, she looked up to the sun every day, thinking, "It's still summer, but autumn is coming soon."

And when autumn came, she thought: "It's still autumn, but soon the cold winter is coming."

She collected even more diligently, allowed no rest until all the pantries were filled.

The other mouse was lazy. She did not get up until the sun was high in the sky. But once she was in the meadow, she felt like dancing. She danced and sang and lived a good life. When the lazy mouse passed the industrious, she called to her: "Come, dance and sing with me!"

But the diligent meadow mouse shouted: "I have no time! I have to collect supplies. »

The warm days passed and it was getting cold. Now the lazy mouse began to gather supplies, but she found only a few grains and nuts.

When it started to snow, sat the diligent mouse in her cave. When she was hungry, she went to one of her pantries and ate her supplies. But soon she got bored. 'If only someone came to visit,' she thought, 'then they could chat together.'

At the same time, the other mouse had eaten all supplies. She sat there starving and freezing and getting weaker and weaker. With the last of her strength, she went to the other mouse's den and said, "Please help me. I'm so hungry. If I do not get something to eat soon, I have to die."

"What about your supplies?" The other mouse asked. "If you had collected as diligently as I did, you would not have to go hungry now!"

"You're right!" Shouted the lazy mouse. "But in the summer, it was so much fun to dance and sing and I forgot to gather for the winter."

The industrious mouse did not want to share her laboriously collected supplies and sent the hungry mouse away. But no sooner had she left, than she was alone again in her cave and bored. Quickly she jumped up, hopped to the other mouse's cave and shouted, "Come on! I'll share my supplies with you, but you've got to dance, sing and chat all winter with me! "

And so both soon sat in the cave and ate seeds and tubers and when they were full, the one mouse began to sing and dance and soon danced the other mouse with.

THE REAR DOOR

Once upon a time there was a woman who had two children. A boy and a girl. One day she went on the journey and said to them, "Listen, children, I am leaving and you are staying home alone. That's why it's a good fit for the rear door. " She meant that they should be careful that no thief creeps in through the rear door.

She had been gone a while, when the two got bored, and the brother said to the nurse: "Come on, we want to go out into the forest a little bit, and we'll take the rear door, then it's good!"

She was satisfied and they went out into the woods. But as they ran around, they got lost and the night overtook them, so they saw that they would not be coming home, and with fear they climbed on an oak tree to stay there until morning so they would not be aware of the wild beasts torn up.

For a while they sat there, thieves came and hauled in a lot of money, they want to count. Since the little ones keep very quiet in the tree, so they are not noticed by the men.

But at last his brother can not keep calm anymore and he says to his sister: "I have to do something small."

"Well, do it!"

There he does it, but the thieves quietly continue their money and say, "It's a little rain falling."

Again after a while the brother says to the sister: "I can not hold it any longer, I have to do something big."

"Well, then do it!"

There he does it, but the thieves quietly continue to count and say, "It's a little crap of the birds sitting in the tree."

Now they sit quietly for a long time, when suddenly the brother says: "I can not hold the rear door anymore."

"So throw her down!" Says the sister.

Then he throws her down and she falls in the midst of the thieves, and they hurry away and shout: "The clouds are falling from the sky, the clouds are falling from the sky!"

Now it was almost morning, and then brother and sister went down from the tree, and took the rear door and the money the thieves had left, and returned home happily.

The mother went to meet them and whined and scolded that they had not taken care of the rear door and now thieves had been there and took everything.

The little ones, however, told everything as they had done in the forest, and there she was glad. And with the money she bought new clothes and new equipment, and there was so much left over that they all had enough of it all their lives.

THE PRINCESS IN THE FLAMMENBURG

Once upon a time there was a poor man who had had as many children as holes in a sieve and all the people in his village as godparents. When he was again born a son, he sat down on the road to ask the first best to be godfather. Then an old man in a gray cloak came to meet him, he asked, and he agreed and went to the baptism. As a baptismal gift, the old man gave the father a cow with a calf. That was born the same day as the boy and had a golden star on his forehead.

The boy grew older and bigger and the calf also grew, became a big bull and the boy led him every day to the mountain meadow. But the bull was able to speak, and when they were on the top of the mountain, the bull spoke: "Stay here and sleep, I want to find my own willow!" As soon as the boy fell asleep, the bull ran like lightning on the big one Sky meadow and eats golden star flowers. When the sun went down, he hurried back, woke the boy, and then they went home. So it happened every day until the boy was twenty years old.

One day the bull spoke to him: "Now sit between my horns, I carry you to the king. Demand from him a seven-meter-long iron sword and tell him that you want to save his daughter. "

Soon they arrived at the castle. The boy dismounted, went to the king and said why he had come. He gladly gave the shepherd boy the required sword. But he had no hope of ever seeing his daughter again. Already many brave youths had tried in vain to rescue them, because a twelve-headed dragon had kidnapped them, and this lived far away, where nobody could get to. First, there was a high, insurmountable mountain on the way there, secondly, a wide and stormy sea, and third, the dragon lived in a castle of flame. If any one had succeeded in crossing the mountains and the sea, he would not have been able to penetrate through the mighty flames, and if he had succeeded, the dragon would have killed him.

When the boy had the sword, he sat down between the horns of the bull, and in no time they were before the great mountain. "Now we have to turn back," he said to the bull, for it seemed impossible for him to get across. But the bull said: "Wait a minute!", Put the boy on the ground, and as soon as that happened, he took a start and pushed with his huge horns the whole mountain on the side.

Now the bull again put the boy between the horns. They moved on and came to the sea. "Now we have to turn back!" Said the boy, "because no one can go over there!"

"Wait a minute," said the bull, "and hold on to my horns."

He bent his head to the water and soffit and sofficated the whole sea, so that they moved on dry feet as in a meadow.

Now they were soon at the Flammenburg. From afar, they were met with such a glow that the boy could not stand it anymore. "Stop!" He shouted to the bull, "no farther, or we'll have to burn." The bull, however, ran very close and poured the sea he had drunk into the flames, so that they soon extinguished and a more powerful one Smoke arose that darkened the whole sky. Then the twelve-headed dragon rushed out of the black clouds angrily.

"Now it's up to you!" Cried the bull to the boy, "make sure you knock all the heads off the monster!" He took all his strength, grasping the mighty sword in both hands, and giving the dragon one like that quick blow that blew all heads off. But now the monster struck and curled on the earth, causing her to tremble. The bull took the dragon's trunk on its horns and hurled it so high up to the clouds, until no trace of it was to be seen.

Then he spoke to the boy: "My service is now over. Now go to the castle, there you will find the princess and lead her home to her father!

"With that he ran away to the sky meadow, and the boy did not see him again. He found the princess, and she was very glad that she was redeemed from the terrible dragon. They drove to their father, held a wedding, and it was a great joy throughout the kingdom.

THE STORY OF THE WISE OWL

Long ago, an owl lived deep in the forest. She nestled in the mighty crown of an oak and listened gladly when the animals of the forest told of their joys and sorrows.

Even the owl liked to tell stories that the wind and the rain had brought her from far away. One day, however, she decided to leave the deep forest and move out to hear new stories.

She spread her wings and flew into the wide world. With her big eyes she saw everything, everything she heard with her sharp ears, and everything kept them carefully in her memory.

So the years went by and the owl got older and wiser. Then she longed for her forest and the big oak tree and she decided to go home.

She flew for many days and nights, until she was silent in the crown of the old Eichelandete.

When the animals of the forest heard that the wise owl had returned, they gathered in the moonlight under the oak and wanted to hear the fairy tales they had brought from the wide world. The owl told such wonderful things that no one wanted to go to sleep.

She put her fairy tales together like pearls on a string, and all the animals listened with bated breath. "How wise you are, Mrs. Owl!" Said a bear after the owl had finished. "I learned so much from you, it's too bad people do not know your fairy tales." The wise owl pondered the bear's words for a long time.

When she felt that she had not much time to live, she took a thick book and a quill pen. She wrote and wrote and wrote, and when she wrote the last story, she closed her eyes forever. But the thick book fell under the oak, and there I found it.

A BRILLIANT FRIEND

It's a beautiful morning on the rider's yard of Mila's parents. Here live Mila, mom, dad and many horses. Mila likes all of them. Even if they are all different. For example, Shooting Star is very meek. At least to Mila. If Dad does not look, she likes to cling to Sternschnuppe's side with her cheek. Karacho, on the other hand, is very boisterous and wild. But Mila is fine too. Every horse is special in its own way.

dAs long as Mila can think she wants her own horse. But Dad always says it's too early. And so she helps her dad to feed the horses on the ranch and has even already mucked out one or the other stall alone.

Today is Mila's seventh birthday. She is very excited and hopes to finally get her own horse. She gets up early and wakes her parents. "I've become seven!" She calls at the foot of the parent's bed. The arms have ripped her high in the air. Mum and dad just rub their eyes sleepily.

Slowly Papa straightens up: "Oh Sparrow, that's right, it's your birthday. I almost forgot that. "Mila looks at him suspiciously:" Did not you! You just want to kid me! "Mila's father laughs:" You've seen through me again! You are very clever. That's what you have to get from your mother. "He says and gives mom a kiss on the cheek - before he gets up.

"I'm sorry," Mila snorts and sticks out her tongue. "Do that when you're alone." Then she whizzes down the stairs and shouts, "Now come on. Time for my birthday breakfast! "When Mila arrives downstairs, she is amazed. Usually, their gifts are always set up on the kitchen table. But today she is standing in front of an empty table.

"Sorry darling!" Dad says as he comes down the stairs. "You're up so early that we did not have time to have breakfast." Mila is now looking under the kitchen table. "What are you doing honey?" Asks dad. Mila's head flits between the table and the chair: "Well, what? Where are my presents? "

Then she pushes the chair jerkily aside and jumps up. Beaming with joy, she calls out to her dad, "I'm finally going to get a horse right?" That's why there are no presents here. "

The dad turns on the coffee machine and turns to Mila: "Honey, you know ..." Mila interrupts him - she knows this sound: "Yes, yes, it is too early for a horse." The father nods. "Right! It's still too early. Now we have breakfast first and then it goes to school. This afternoon we pick up your horse.

Mila did not really listen to her dad, "Everytime you say it's too early. But I take care of the horses and they all love me. I've never ridden before, but I've cleaned out all the stables, all the horses ... "Mila stops and listens:" Did you just say ... "Mila's father nods. "You little chatterbox. Has it reached you now? "He asks. But Mila storms towards him and falls into his arms. Meanwhile, Mama has come down and hugs both. "Did your dad tell you so?" She says, kissing Mila's head.

At school, Mila can hardly concentrate. Thousands of questions go through her mind. What does your horse look like? How should she get on the horse's back - as small as she is? Mila can not wait to get home. When the bell sounds at the end of the last hour, she has already packed everything and runs off like an oiled lightning.

When she reaches home, she immediately runs to her father's stable. "I'm there. We can go. "She puffs her out of breath. She has run all the way. "Man Mila," laughs the father. "Get some air. You're pumping like a cockchafer. "Mila has to reach down to her hips and bend her knees to catch her breath - she's out of breath. "That's OK. Get the keys. I'm waiting for the car. "

The dad puts the food bag aside. "We do not need to leave. I had some time this morning, so I've already got your pony. "Mila is suddenly just like a one. Her gaze wanders off the stables. There is only one box that has been empty for a long time. Immediately Mila whizzes away again. But the box is still empty. "Where is it?" She calls.

"The pony is on the big pasture." Replies the father. The big willow. This means the large flower meadow above the stream. Mila can barely walk. Nevertheless, she gives everything and sprints off. Her dad is struggling to come after her. On the way to the pasture, she thinks. "Daddy said pony. I'm worried about that. "She thinks and is happy. "I should go up to a pony."

At the top of the pasture, Mila stops dead. There is her pony. At last! It looks like a shrunken Haflinger. It has a white, shaggy mane, a white, shaggy tail and is light brown all over. Only in the face it has a white spot. It's perfect!

Dad comes with a food bag in his hand. "Well, how do you like it?" He asks softly. "It's perfect," she whispers, squeezing him tightly. "The blaze on the face is very sweet." Mila pulls a carrot out of the bag and lures her pony with it. The pony cautiously sniffs it. The nostrils go very far, but it does not eat the carrot. Instead, the pony sniffs at Mila's dad.

Mila is disappointed: "Is not she hungry?" She asks her father. But at the same moment, the pony grabs the food bag from his father's hand. Then it turns around and wants to go to a pen. Mila laughs out loud.

"Hey you naughty badger!" Calls Mila's dad and quickly reaches for the reins. Mila is excited: "Did you see that? That was pretty smart! "Mila's dad laughs:" Of course I've seen that. "Then he reaches for the food bag and takes it away from the pony again. "But you're right, that was a brilliant move!"

Mila looks at her dad. "I think he did not like it that much." She laughs. "What's the name of my pony?" Mila's daddy brings the food pouch to safety. "Your pony is a he. And his name is Brilliant, "he says.

Mila shines all over her face: "The name fits like a pot on a lid!" "Like the lid on the pot, you mean." Mila's dad corrects. "Yes, that's what I mean!" Replies Mila. "And now? Am I finally learning to ride? Should I ever climb the pony? "

"Not so hasty!" Says Mila's dad. "No one has ridden on Brilliant yet. You're the first. "Mila jumps up and down with joy and claps her hands. She is so happy that she can hardly stand it.

Mila's dad is getting serious now. "Listen to my little one. Riding a horse is something for experienced riders. If Brilliant gets used to you from the beginning, your new friend needs to learn to fully trust you."

Mila has also calmed down now. "I understand that, Dad." She says. She thinks of the other horses in the barn and how it was when she first had to curry Karacho. She had to be very careful. Karacho is very spirited and he was very restless; until he got used to Mila.

Mila slowly approaches the Brilliant with the carrot. Brilliant tilts a bit unsteadily with his hooves, as if he is considering what he should think of it. But the scent of carrots triumphs. Carefully, he bites off the carrot. While chewing, Mila gently puts her hand on his forehead. Brilliant closes his eyes for a moment. As if he enjoys the touch.

Finally, Mila puts her hand on his neck. "Quiet my friend," she says and feeds him on. "You're doing really well!" Praises Mila's dad softly. After a short time Mila can stroke her pony on the back. And then slip on the other side even under the neck, without Brilliant recoiling. As a reward, there is an apple directly from the tree.

As it turns out, Brilliant loves apples. Because when he sees the apple, he immediately begins to scrape excitedly with his hooves and snort. Mila loves apples too. So Mila takes the first bite and Brilliant gets the rest.

While Brilliant is still enjoying chewing, Mila strokes his forehead again and whispers: "We are becoming the best friends. Is it Brilliant?

And best friends share everything. "Brilliant lowers his head and Mila gently places her cheek on his forehead. Brilliant steals Mila again and again easily.

Mila's dad can hardly believe it. He wanted to say something when Mila put her cheek on Brilliant's forehead. But then he saw this intimacy between the two and could not imagine that Brilliant Mila would ever do anything.

The sun is already low and Mila's dad calls her that it's already late. Mila takes Brilliant by the reins and leads him from the pasture into the stable. Brilliant Mila trots all the way left behind.

When Brilliant is standing in his box, Daddy Mila strokes her cheek and says, "Now you're going to eat supper and get you ready for bed, okay? The mom is already waiting. And tomorrow we go on. "Mila nods, squeezes her dad and gives Brilliant another kiss on the forehead:" Sleep well my friend. "She whispers and clings to him again.

Then she walks in to Mama and tells her about her great day at supper. Before going to bed, she presses her mom again firmly and thanks for the wonderful birthday. As much as Mila has experienced today, she does not even need a good night

THE HARE PIRATES ON A TREASURE HUNT

It is a beautiful day. There is not a single cloud in the sky far and wide. On the shallow water a pirate ship crosses across the sea.

The sun shines on the sailor. But there is no time for laze. On the ship is once again looking diligently for a treasure island. Because the pirates thirst for gold and jewels.

The helmsman still does not know exactly where the journey should go. Because so far the pirates sail only on the basis of a half treasure map. To find the treasure, you must first look for the other half of the treasure map.

But now there is another problem for now. At the stern of the ship an octopus has settled. That slows down the whole ride. The captain takes a short piece of wood and heads for the octopus. Then he throws the wood as far as he can into the sea. He calls out loud and the octopus jumps from the stern into the water and swims behind the stick. "Well, then you go water-terrier!" The captain whispers in his beard before he goes back to the treasure hunt.

And there it sounds already from the lookout tower: "Land ahead! Hard port! "The captain pushes the helmsman aside and tears the helm around with a grin. In front of them an island appears on the horizon. Is this the treasure island? Hard to say without the second part of the map. But it's a start. Hustle is spreading on the pirate ship. The sails are reset quickly. Every hare on board hurries as best he can. Why the rabbits are so hectic you ask?

Well, they are not the only ones looking for the treasure. Other pirates have sneaked the first part of the treasure map and are now looking for wealth and honor.

One evening, the captain's right paw - the lanky Hellgard Hüpfer - was not paying close attention and fell asleep while the treasure map was lying on his bedside table. This moment was maliciously exploited. A devious pirate sneaked into the sleeping chamber of the captain's right paw to secretly draw the treasure map. And now the pirates are in competition with the insidious villains. First come first serve.

True, the Pirates Code does not prohibit treacherously providing an advantage; but he commands the one who finds him first.

The island is getting closer and the lookout is getting loud. "Second part of the treasure map ahead!" Willi gets far-sighted and falls from sheer excitement almost from the observation deck. Phew, that just went well.

When the captain hears the call, he does not trust his eavesdroppers. He rushes to the railing of the pirate ship and reaches for the telescope. "Where? Where? "He exclaims excitedly. But then he sees something that makes his blood freeze in his veins.

The second part of the treasure map is in a bottle post. But this was already fished out of the sea The captain sees the unbelievable in the distance. "Ai Potz flash. Someone fries an Easter egg for me. This is a Meerjungzibbe holds the Boddel. "Poltert it from the nose of the captain.

And indeed. On the island sits a mermaid, er, sorry, baby boy - as the captain already said - and holds the message in his paws.

There is caution. Because, as the captain already really rumbles on: "With Meerjungzibben is not jut cherries eat mi Jung!"

And he orders the sailor to catch up with the sails and slow down.

Then he roars with all his might: "Guns starboard!" All sailors hurry frantically. Then the cannons are dragged to starboard. The sailors sing in rhythm: "And one and draw and one and move ..."

The ship swings from left to right, from right to left. It rocks so hard that some cannons roll back by themselves. "Ai pats again! Just stay a while! "Cries the young Torben dub, as he is pulled by a cannon across the deck.

With all his might he tries to hold the monster. But there is nothing to do. The cannon continues indefatigably on its way. To make matters worse, he stumbles over a plank and flies in a high arc on the rolling cannon.

Now both of them dash past the other pirates with Karacho. Two sailors can take cover at the last moment before the cannon with a bang and the poor Torben dub with a dull - PATSCH - crash against the gang of the ship.

The other sailors can hardly keep from laughing. "That was a clean crash landing, mi Jung! These are cannons and not horses! "The laughter breaks out of the thick pirate Kunjard sausage.

"Well wait," thinks Torben dub and gets up. When he has the cannon back in the right place he deliberately jumps on the tube as if he wants to ride the monster. Then he grabs the fuse, lights the fire and gets ready.

When all the cannons are aligned, the ship is close enough to the island to deliver the first salvo. Now the other pirates ignite the blazing fire and get ready.

"Fire free!" Thundered the captain's powerful voice over the planks. The Lunten are ignited and with a deafening roar hurl the cannon balls from the steel pipes into the open air.

The cannons bounce a bit backwards. Torben dumbs up an arm and yells, "Jiiihah." Sitting on the cannon like a cowboy doing a rodeo.

The other sailors and pirates marvel not bad at the daring pirate boys. Especially not when they see Torben's butt caught fire. Everyone looks at him with big eyes.

Torben himself does not notice and sits proudly like Oskar on the cannon. "N / A? You did not think so, did you? "He boasts. But then he perceives the smell of burnt fur.

He sniffs and sniffs - looks around - and keeps sniffing. "What is it that offends my sense of smell?" He asks when suddenly he discovers the fire on his bottom.

He jumps frantically into the next water barrel. After a loud "Splash Pffffffffff" you can only see steam rising. Soaking wet, the poor dork sits in the barrel. And everyone can laugh heartily again.

In the meantime the mermaid has heard the tremendous bang and jumped in the water. The bottle post with the second part of the treasure map has dropped her.

When the pirate Marla Mutig saw this, she jumped boldly over the plank to get the Boddel. Now she is also spotted by the lookout. "Hare overboard!" Calls Willi Weitsicht just when he suddenly notices that one of the insidious treasure map thieves sneaks over the main sail.

Down on deck, meanwhile, a large piece of wood is flying past the captain's head. Amazed, he turns around and sees the octopus from earlier. Apparently she has found the stick and wants the captain to throw it again.

Meanwhile, standing on the mast now the rogue with drawn saber directly in front of Willi Weitsicht and mumbled: "I make you shish kebab on the spit." But there it rang from the deck: "Sails clear her water rats!" Bellowed the captain.

He had long since noticed the other pirate ship and does not hesitate to fire long. Immediately the sailors clear the sails and the attacker is swept off the main mast like spinach from the kitchen table. The rogue lands in the sea with a belly slapper.

The octopus jumps happily afterwards. She probably thinks the villain is a stick. You do not want to get stuck in his skin now. It only takes a moment and the rogue flies screaming over the pirate ship. The octopus thought it was too good with the momentum.

After the rogue has flown past the captain, he grabs the telescope and searches in the distance for Marla Mutig in the water. He can not find her.

"Marla come on - where are you? A water rat like you is not drowned, "he whispers to himself. The captain knows they have to hurry if they want to find the treasure first. And there Marla Mutig is his best chance.

The captain can not find the pirate in the water at all. For now she has collected the bottle post and has swum to the island. She just wants to open the message in the bottle when she sees it.

Just within reach, suddenly everything seems in vain. The second part of the map is no longer legible. The mermaid had opened the message in the bottle before leaping into the water. Now the treasure map is saturated with salt water. All the ink has gone and the treasure seems lost.

Marla stares at the card and falls to her knees. Was everything else now? The salt water on the treasure map is now joined by Marla's tears. She is sobbing and crying. Should everything really be over now?

But as luck would have it, there is a happy ending. Because when Marla looks up, she sees the treasure chest standing right in front of her. The mermaid had already found the treasure. She sat on it just before, without the pirate noticing.

Marla Mutig wipes away her tears and retrieves the golden key from the bottle. Then she puts him in the lock of the chest - the key fits. With a "crack" the lock opens. That's the end of the race - because the Pirate Code rules, who found it first, can keep it.

The captain has now also spotted Marla Mutig and the treasure on the island and shouts to the crew: "We have found the treasure! Today there are carrots for everyone and in abundance! "The pirates jump joyfully up and down.

The insidious villains, however, do not look very happy. According to the Pirate Codex, you lost the race for the treasure. And so they leave untapped things and no prey.

Marla has meanwhile ransacked the treasure chest. The box contains bags of gold, jewelery and jewelery. Most notable, however, is a ring with a diamond twice as large as Marla's paw.

When the other pirates finally reach the island, the joy is still great! It is cheered and celebrated until the sun goes down. Once again a treasure was found. Only the ring with the big diamond has disappeared. Well, who has that?

SOMETHING IS DIFFERENT

Hannah wakes up one morning and something is funny. Something feels different than usual. But what is it? Hannah looks around. Everything is in its place. The night light is on the bedside table and Bruno is sitting on the floor next to the bed.

Bruno is Hannah's favorite stuffed animal. A little white dog with a straw hat and dungarees. For a long time Bruno slept in bed. But Hannah is growing and so is not as much space in bed as before. In addition, Hannah is firmly convinced that Bruno has told her that he prefers to take care of her at night instead of sleeping. And that's a good thing - think Hannah!

Hannah slips off the bed, barefoot on the carpet. The carpet also feels as it always has. Funny! But no matter, Hannah thinks. She grabs Bruno under the arm and runs to mom and dad in the bedroom.

With a proper jump she jumps into the parents' bed and shouts, "Get up! I'm awake!". Hannah's mom and dad are still very sleepy. "Are you hungry honey?" Mum asks. Hannah thinks. "Hm, I think I could eat pancakes." Mum laughs: "We can not quite do it my darling. Today is kindergarten again. But tomorrow is the weekend. I'd like to make some pancakes for you. "

Hannah snaps her arms up: "Yes, weekend and pancakes." Then she jumps off the bed. "Come on Mom. We make breakfast fast and then kindergarten. Then it's really weekend! "

On the way to the kitchen Hannah tells her mom what happened today - that anything feels weird. Mom touches Hannah's forehead. "Hm. So - you do not have a fever. Take A. "Hannah opens her mouth wide and sticks out her tongue:" Ahhhhhhh. "But Mom shakes her head. "Everything's fine, too," she says.

As Hannah bites into the breakfast sandwich, she is startled. "Ow!" She calls. "What's up?" Mum asks. Hannah touches her finger in her mouth. "Hoa." She says with her finger in her mouth. Then she pulls out her finger. "There's a tocth wobbling!" She says indignantly.

Mama smiles: "Oh, you have a wiggle tooth. That explains a lot. Show me. "But Hannah quickly closes her mouth and shakes her head. Then she says, "No! I do not want to go to the dentist. "Mama strokes her cheek. "Darling, you do not have to go to the dentist with a wiggle."

Hannah makes big eyes. "Not?" She asks. "No!" Says Mom. "A jiggle falls out by itself. And when the time comes, we put it under your pillow at night. "" Ieeeee! "Interrupts Hannah's mom. "I'm not putting my tooth under my pillow."

Again, the mother smiles and says: "But only then can the tooth fairy get him. The next morning the tooth is gone and there is a coin there. "Hannah looks at Mum in disbelief. "Why is that?" She asks. "Because the tooth fairy does it," Mama answers.

Hannah does not quite understand that. "A fairy fetches my tooth and gives me money for it?" That makes Hannah think. "How much do I get for a tooth?" And immediately her finger disappears in her mouth again. "Uond waviel teeth hoeh ich then?"

"Enough to get rich," Mom jokes. But Hannah does not take that as a joke. "I knew it!" She calls and rubs her hands.

At kindergarten, Hannah eagerly talks about the Tooth Fairy. Jonas says tiredly: "Oh, about Zahr.fee. This is definitely a mouse that steals the tooth. "But what does Jonas know? Jonas is stupid, thinks Hannah.

"Not at all!" Sandra intervened suddenly. "I've already put a tooth under my pillow and the next day there was money and the tooth was gone. So! "Then Jonas sticks out her tongue:" Bäääääh! "

Nevertheless, Hannah's sentence does not go out of her mind all day long. When Daddy picks up Hannah, she folds her arms and says, "I do not want a mouse to go under my pillow." Daddy looks at Hannah in amazement. "What mouse?" He asks. "Well, the tooth mouse." Hannah answers precociously. "Jonas says there is no tooth fairy. If I put my wiggle tooth under my pillow, then a mouse comes and fetches it. "

"Oh, Hannah," Dad says. "There is no tooth mouse! Do not listen to everything that's being told. "Hannah's stomach growls as loud as a bear. "Have not you eaten anything?" Dad asks in astonishment. Hannah turns away: "When I eat, my tooth falls out and then the mouse comes!"

Hannah's dad squats down and nudges Hannah. "The only mouse here is you," he whispers. "If your tooth is under the pillow, there comes a beautiful tiny little fairy. She is very happy about your tooth. And because you no longer need him, she buys him from you. That's all."

Hannah turns to her daddy: "And you are quite sure?" Hannah's father smiles and nudges her again: "Absolutely!" He says in a firm voice. "Alright! Then I want a huge dinner now. "Says Hannah and pulls her arms apart.

A few days later, it is actually time. Hannah's Wackelzahn finally falls out while eating. Hannah is really excited. She was never as fast at bed-making as she is today. When Mama says good night and begins to read a story, Hannah is fidgeting all the time. "What's going on?" Asks Hannah's mom. "I do not know exactly where to put my tooth down," she says restlessly, holding up her wobble tooth.

Hannah's mom takes the tooth and puts it under the pillow. "Well my sweatheart. Here he is exactly right. But now listen to the story and then sleep well. Because the fairy only comes when you sleep. "Hannah nods and listens to the story. "I can not sleep tonight," she thinks. But before she knows it, she has already fallen asleep.

The next morning she wakes up and slides barefoot on the floor. When she feels the carpet, she suddenly remembers the wobbly tooth. She quickly reaches for the pillow to check. The tooth is actually gone. She pulls the pillow off the bed and at the same moment she hears something falling on the carpet - a coin. She looks at the coin in amazement and whispers: "The tooth fairy was there." Then she grabs the money and runs happily to her parents. Again and again she calls, "They exist. Look, they really exist! "She runs straight into her daddy's arms. "Ui, with so much energy." Dad says as he takes Hannah up. Mom is making breakfast. "I said that," she laughs.

Hannah struggles with her legs. This is the sign for dad to let her down again. Once at the bottom, she stands straight up and holds the coin up. "I will show Jonas. He l look around, "she says cheekily and everyone laughs heartily.

Then Hannah thinks for a moment and says: "Do you know what? I will always put all my wobbly teeth under my pillow. And when I'm rich, we all go ice cream! "Mom and Dad think the idea is great, and Hannah is proud to have lost her first shaky tooth - or rather, to have sold!

BAGGI'S UNWANTED SLIDE

Baggi loves to dig big holes. For that Baggi is still such a small excavator, he is already really fast. Once he grows up, he wants to be as big and strong a digger as his dad. The dredge huge pile of soil and debris in no time from one end of the construction site to another. The construction workers needed it for days. A strong excavator, like Baggis Papa, can do it in a few hours.

Baggi likes helping his dad with digging and so he has been to construction sites often. So often that he knows the environment like his own shovel. But that does not mean that things do not go wrong again and again.

Today, a house is to be built. For that the construction workers need a big hole in the earth. Said and done. Baggi gets going. Although he can dig really fast, he has to work hard to keep up with his daddy. Shovel by shovel, the hole grows larger quickly. Shovel after shovel but it is also fast deep. Baggi is so energetic and anxious to show his father what he is capable of, that he becomes overzealous.

He rolls faster and faster between the dug earth and the hole. It starts to drizzle. Baggis dad calls for a bad-weather break immediately - because safety first! But Baggi is at it right now and does not dream of stopping now.

But the wetter the earth gets, the slipperier it will be. Suddenly Baggi starts to skid. With momentum he rushes towards the hole. Even frightened by the unwanted slide and full of effort the little Baggi tries to slow down. But once you're in the slip, even the best brake will not help.

Baggi has an idea. He pushes his little shovel with all his strength into the ground. Now he is pulling a deep furrow and an ever-increasing pile of mud behind him. So the little Baggi tries to brake. And his plan seems to work out too, because he is getting bit by bit slower.

But unfortunately he came too late to this brilliant idea, because on the edge of the hole he is now on the loose and desperately trying to shift his weight forward so as not to slip into the huge hole.

Baggis slide was so fast that Baggis dad had not heard the fast-paced drama. Seeing Baggi on the tip, he rushes to his son's aid immediately. The wet ground does not make it easy for him. And so he comes to a tire length too late. Directly in front of him the small excavator slides straight into the hole. Behind him slips the wet earth, which he had accumulated during the slide.

Smudged and smudged with mud and earth, the little excavator now squats in the huge hole. As much as he tries to come out again, he finds no support. The wheels spin in the wet soil and he digs deeper into the earth. Even his strong dad can not reach him now.

"Just stay calm my boy. We'll get you out of there! "Shouts Baggis dad. Then he looks up and sees the construction workers standing on the other side of the hole. They are sprinkled with mud from top to bottom. Baggi had been so eager to get out of the hole that the mud had flown in a high arc to the construction workers. These now stand like drowned poodles on the edge and wipe the muddy ground from the face.

But on the job site, fortunately, one is a big family and not at all resentful. Because especially during construction can go something wrong. The important thing is that you help each other then.

The foreman taps the dirt from the radio. Then he immediately informs the crane driver: "Excavator in need!". The crane operator sees what is going on and swings the crane over the hole to free Baggi from his predicament.

Happy to have solid ground under the wheels, Baggi is relieved. But he is also embarrassed. For one thing, he should have listened to the security regulations and thus his dad. And on the other hand, everyone will surely make fun of him and tell funny stories about him.

But to Baggis astonishment no one makes fun of him. But on the contrary. Everyone is really worried about the little excavator and asks him if everything is alright and how it happened? Baggi tells the story from the beginning. After a while, he realizes that he is telling a funny story about himself. And that is really funny! The construction workers have a lot of fun listening to Baggis story. And since it is raining right now, no more work is done today anyway. But still laughed a lot and Baggi laughs heartily with! One bed free and one for three?

Today I tell you a story about a little girl named Lydia. Lydia is 4 years old and always nice and good. Mom and Dad are very proud that they have such a sweet child. Mum often even says "My Angel" to Lydia, because she is as good as an angel. But there is one thing that mom and dad do not find so divine. Lydia sleeps in her parents' bed every night.

How come? Surely you are asking yourself now. Does not she have her own bed? But she has. And even a very cuddly. With many stuffed animals and a lot of space for such a little girl as Lydia. But Lydia just does not want to sleep in her own bed. She finds it much more comfortable with mom and dad.

At the same time, Lydia does not know what it's like to sleep in her own bed. That was so long ago that she forgot.

Mom and dad love Lydia very much. But as big as mom and daddy's bed is, it's a little tight for three. Especially since Lydia gets bigger and bigger. When the dad turns around at night, he nudges Lydia. Then Lydia awakens briefly and turns around too. She bumps into her mom and the mom is awake and turns around. And when dad turns around again, the game starts again.

Sometimes Lydia twitches in her sleep. She then dreams something and begins to fidget with her arms and legs. Lydia herself does not notice. But depending on how she's lying, either mom or dad is lucky enough to get hit. Of course one wakes up on it. And if you do not sleep enough, you are not well rested in the morning.

If Lydia wants to play during the day, mom and dad are way too broken. You did not sleep much. And it was exhausting enough to do the work and the household.

Lydia thinks that's stupid. The solution would be so simple. She would only have to sleep in her own bed. Then mom and dad would have slept well and cheerful enough to play with Lydia.

Lydia used to sleep in her own bed when she was younger. There she liked to cuddle with her teddy. But Lydia does not remember that. At some point she got a new bed - because she got bigger. And she did not sleep once in the new bed.

If Mama Lydia had asked her if she would like to sleep in her own bed, then Lydia said, "No." Lydia said more. But today Mama said something for the first time that made Lydia think. "Your teddy is certainly very sad and misses you very doll."

Lydia did not even think that when she sleeps with Mom and Dad, her stuffed animals are all alone. And indeed, her stuffed animals were already very sad. The little brown teddy, her doll, the white rabbit Mr. Schlappohr and her little pink unicorn were all alone. Of course, that had to be changed immediately.

As Mama was packing laundry in the bedroom, Lydia scurried past her. The stuffed animals in her arms. Lydia placed the cuddly toys on Mom's and Dad's bed and said, "Problem solved." Then she rubbed her hands like daddy when he finished something.

Mama did not have that in mind when she told Lydia about the sad stuffed animals. She knelt down in front of Lydia and said, "My angel. Thats not OK. So we do not have enough space in the bed. We can hardly sleep that way."

Lydia thought for a moment. That's right, there was another problem. Mom and Dad were always too tired. Should she try to sleep in her own bed? Discouraged, she breathed out, "Phew. You and Dad are so far away. "She said. Mom looked at Lydia, "You mean when you sleep in your bed?" "Yes!" Lydia answered.

Now Mom thought, "Hm." Then she said, "What do you think if we leave your door a bit open. And we also leave ours a bit open. Then we'll hear you immediately, if anything should be. "

Lydia looked incredulous. But mom had an idea. "We'll try that out right away. That will be fun. What do you say? "Lydia nodded and ran to her room," Hello Mom! "She exclaimed. And mom answered, "Hello Lydia, my angel!" It actually worked. Lydia could hear Mama without Mom having to scream. So the two spent a while and made all sorts of funny sounds that the other had to guess.

When Dad came home, he went with him immediately. Now Mama called from the bedroom, Lydia from the nursery and dad from the room. That was funny. But dad had also brought two surprises.

Once a totally cuddly blanket and a great nightlight. The blanket was pink. Because Lydia loves pink. There were also little flowers on it, which almost looked like starlets. Asterisks would have preferred Lydia, but the flowers glowed in the dark and that was great.

The nightlight actually made little stars. If you turned it on, there were little glowing stars all over the nursery. When Dad said that the night light is extra for the night and allowed to stay all night, Mama immediately said, "Well, you see. Not only can you hear us, you can see everything in your room at night."

Now Lydia liked her room a lot better. And mom also had some news. Because if Lydia slept in her own bed now, then she was already big and brave. That's why Lydia was allowed to stay awake 15 minutes longer every evening. Lydia was happy and she felt really grown up.

After supper Lydia got ready for bed. From the bathroom she marched straight into Mom's and Dad's bedroom. What was going on now? Lydia wanted to sleep in her own bed today. Oh well, the stuffed animals were still there. Well, they had to be fetched, of course.

Then Lydia cuddled up with the new blanket in her cot. Teddy, Mr. Schlappohr, her doll and her unicorn around. The great nightlight sparkled and Mama read her another story. This Lydia could fall asleep really nice. She was sound asleep. And she even dreamed something nice.

DADDY THE TOO MUMBEARD

'll tell you the story of Eduard today. Eduard is a sheep. But not just any sheep, no. Eduard is a dream sheep. What a dream sheep is you asking? If you close the dead and count sheep at night, then Eduard is the number seven dream sheep that jumps over the fence.

As a dream sheep with the number seven, but he has not so much to do. Often the children already sleep at sheep number four or five. That's why Eduard is often bored. But he is at least the replacement sheep for number five. So if sheep number five is ill or on vacation, then Eduard may jump over the fence twice. One fifth and one seventh.

But Eduard then has to hurry up doll. Because if he jumped as a fifth sheep, he must run back behind the meadow very quickly, while sheep number six jumps, and then jump again as the seventh sheep. And he has to run crouched so that the children will not see him. Otherwise you would know that a sheep is missing. And then they could not fall asleep so well.

Eduard would like sheep number one or two - which sheep would not like to be number one or two. Then he would be much better known and have more to do. Hardly anyone knows him as sheep number seven. And how should his work be acknowledged and valued if he barely jumps?

But nevertheless Eduard is glad. It could be far worse. Imagine he was sheep number nine or even sheep number eleven. Not to imagine how boring that would be. Then he would almost never jump. No, only the very lazy sheep can be taken for the sheep number eleven. The ones who sleep a lot anyway.

But no matter, it does not use anything. At the moment, Eduard is looking forward to his vacation. Because once a year, every dream sheep flies on vacation. Of course not all at once. That would be a disaster. Then suddenly the children could not fall asleep so well. No, every dream sheep flies individually on vacation and has a representation.

Eduard likes to fly to the moon on vacation. And so he does it again this time. He sits there for hours and watches the stars. He is happy about every shooting star he sees. Every time he closes his eyes tight and wants something.

When he has just closed his eyes, he suddenly hears something of the earth. In the nurseries all over the world, parents and children talk uninterruptedly. How can that be? It's already bedtime! Eduard thinks and listens more closely.

"Dad, there's something wrong," says a boy. "There's a sheep missing!" "Oh nonsense." Answers the daddy. "You just have to look right." But the boy stays with it. "No dad. Something is missing. I can not sleep like that! "

Eduard also hears such conversations from other children's rooms. "Mum, there's no sheep left? Where is the sheep? "" No, my sparrow. That can not be. Take a closer look. "" Alright. "The little girl answers and wrinkles her nose. "I'll take a close look now." "And?" Mom asks. "Wait, now the other sheep are jumping."

Eduard dawns bad. Oh dear, he thinks. Something is wrong here. And indeed, the number nine sheep that was supposed to jump in for Eduard got sick. Now sheep number eleven jumps in for sheep number nine, but nobody jumps in for Eduard. So there's a yawning void in the sheep between sheep number six and sheep number eight. That's never happened.

Immediately, Eduard jumps into the rocket and dives back to earth. Once there, he jumps into the dream teleporter and "Zoooom" he is back in dreamland. Very quickly he resumes his work as a dream sheep and the children around the world are relieved.

In a nursery one hears: "Mum, there is the sheep again. It's back! "" Well, you see my sparrow. I said that. You just have to look right, then it is there too.

From another nursery one hears: "It was really not there Dad." "Of course it was there. You just did not look right. But now you are sleeping. Good night!"

"Oh dear parents, if only you knew," Eduard thinks. "But no matter. Me and my friends are bringing your kids into sweetest dreams now! Good night and good sleep. Your Eduard the seventh dream sheep. "

A SNOWMAN SAVES CHRISTMAS

Once upon a time there was a snowman who lived in the Christmas wonderland high on a hill in a house sitting on a tree. It was not a tree house. It was a real house in a tree. It was normal in the Christmas Wonderland. There were also gingerbread houses, huge Christmas trees and much more fantastic.

But let's get back to our snowman, whose biggest wish was to be a Christmas elf. However, only elves were allowed to be Christmas Elves. It was written in the big Christmas book.

Nevertheless, the snowman tried it year after year. He disguised himself once as elf to get into the magnificent Christmas factory. But he already noticed the guard on the gate. Maybe his carrot had betrayed him on the face? Or maybe he was just more spherical than anyone else.

It would work this year. Because the snowman had a great idea. He wanted to pack presents himself and distribute them to the children. But could Santa not be angry with him? And he could finally conjure the longed-for smile into the faces of the children.

First, the gifts had to come from. But where to take and not steal? He had to make some money somehow. But what should he do? He sled incredibly well on the sled. But you could not earn money with that.

He remembered something. He slid happily and started to make little snowballs. Then he took a sign and sat down in the snow. On the sign it was written: "Every Ball 3 Taler". That would have to work. Everyone likes snowball fights. But the snowman was sitting in vain hour after hour. Nobody even bought a snowball.

So he asked the blacksmith if he could help. He only laughed loudly. "What do you want to help me with?" The blacksmith asked. "If you stand by the fire with me, you'll melt. Do you want to serve me as drinking water? "

"That's right." Thought the snowman. It had to be something cold. So he went to the ice factory. There large blocks of ice were made to build igloos. But even here, the snowman was laughed at. "How do you want to help me?" Asked the factory manager. "The blocks are so heavy, if you want to push them, break your thin stick sleeves."

"That's right." Thought the snowman again. It has to be something where it's cold and the work is not too hard. So the snowman went to the ice cream seller. He was taken with the idea and said: "You are certainly a good ice cream seller! You're never too cold, and if ice is missing for cooling, we'll just take something from you. "

When the snowman heard that, he was startled. "Ice cream from me?" He asked. "I think I was wrong in the door," he said and walked quickly away.

Now the snowman was sad. Nothing he tried worked. He sank to the ground in the middle of the city. His hat slipped over his sad button eyes. He picked up his violin and played a Christmas carol. That always helped him when he was sad.

As he played, he was so lost in thought that he did not notice the passing people throwing him some change. Only when a stranger passed in said: "A wonderful Christmas carol. That's one of my favorites. Keep playing snowman. "He listened.

He pushed his hat up and saw the change in front of him. "That's money!" He said softly. And played on. "That's money!" He shouted loudly and kept playing. He grinned all over his face and sang with his heart's content: "Tomorrow children will give something. Tomorrow we will be happy ... "

With the newly earned money, he bought gifts and wrapping paper. A doll there and a car here. Hardworking was packed and laced. And the cord passed through the hole. "One right, one left - yes the snowman comes and brings it!"

But wait. How should the presents reach the children from here? The snowman considered. "I can not wear it. But I do not have a Christmas sleigh either. And Santa will hardly lend me his. Besides, the reindeer would want to eat my carrot. "

The snowman could sled incredibly well on a sledge, but it was not always just mountain off. So what to do? Again, the snowman had a great idea. He tied the presents to a snail. Snails can carry a lot. That would work.

Just when he was done, a Christmas elf passed by. "What will that be when it's done?" The Christmas elf asked. The snowman stood proudly next to his snail. "This is my Christmas slug! And I'm giving presents to the children this year. "

The Christmas elf looked at the snowman and the snail in wonderment. "I would laugh now, if it were not so sad," he said then. "You know that a snail is way too slow to deliver gifts to all the children in the world? I mean, she herself would be too slow to supply just this village. "

The happy grin passed by the snowman and the elf continued: "In addition, unfortunately, these are not enough gifts. You would need a million billion more. But it does not matter anyway. Anyway, Christmas is out this year! "

When the snowman heard that, he no longer understood the world. "Christmas is out? That does not work! "The Christmas elf nodded:" And if that works. Santa Claus got sick and can not distribute presents. "

"Naaaein", the snowman breathed in astonishment and looked at the elf in disbelief. "Santa Claus can not get sick." The Christmas elf nodded again: "That's right. Usually not. But this year it's so cold that even our Christmas elves are too cold. "The snowman got nervous:" But Christmas, so Christmas ... so, what about Christmas? "He ran around hectic and talked to himself:" No, no, no, no, that can not be. A Christmas without presents is not a Christmas. "

The Christmas elf interrupted the snowman. "Christmas is very Christmas without gifts. The presents were getting more and more and almost too much over the last few years anyway. "The snowman collapsed briefly and breathed out," Yeah, yaaaaaaaaaa, that's alright. "Then he stood straight up and said," But with presents it's a lot more beautiful."

The Christmas elf shook his head: "Christmas is the festival of charity. No need for presents. "The snowman whirled around and said quietly," Yes, that's right. "Then he took one of his presents and held it up to the Christmas elf's nose." But look how beautiful the presents are. With such a gift, I can show my charity much better than without. "

Then he let the gift disappear behind his back and looked at the Christmas elf sadly. "Look, now it's gone. Is not that sad? Imagine the many little sad googly eyes standing in front of a Christmas tree, under which there are no presents. And now tell the children that we do not need presents, because Christmas is the feast of charity! "

The Christmas elf said, "Okay, maybe you're right. But what should we do? It's too cold! "The snowman tossed the gift aside and slid to the Christmas elf:" Ha! Exactly! It's too cold! ... for Santa Claus. But I'm a snowman! "Then he turned in a circle and began to sing:" I'm never too cold, I'll be so old. I can hurry and hurry, distribute gifts to children. All you have to do is help me with stuff and team. Take me to Santa Claus quickly. "

The Christmas elf covered its ears: "Now stop singing. I'll take you there already. "The snowman jumped in the air with joy:" Juhu! Hey, that was almost rhyming. You could also sing a song. "And so the snowman talked a long while on the way to Santa - to the chagrin of the Christmas Elf.

Arrived at Santa Claus, he was very surprised to see a snowman at home. Usually there were only Christmas elves. But Santa Claus loved the idea that Christmas should not be canceled. Because he was of the opinion that Christmas is simply nicer with gifts. But how should the snowman distribute so many presents?

The snowman chewed nervously on his lips. He was so close to living his biggest dream. "We do not have to distribute all presents," he said. "Everyone gets a little less this year. It's still better than nothing, is not it? "Santa looked at the snowman:" I do not think that's a bad idea. That should work! But how do you want to drive the presents? You can not have my sled! "

The snowman was on the verge of despair. "Only solve this one problem and my dream comes true." He thought. Then he said sheepishly, "Well, I'm a pretty good sledger!" And looked questioningly at Santa. The Christmas elf intervened: "Oh, that's all nonsense! Then you only supply the children who live at the bottom of a mountain? Or how should I imagine that? "

But Santa raised his hand and moved his fingers as if he were scratching the air. Out of nowhere a huge snow slide emerged under the snowman. Then Santa said, "You're such a good sledger. This snow mountain will accompany you. He is a never ending snow slope. So you can go sledding anywhere. "

The snowman looked at the huge snow mountain and said: "That .... Is ... "he suddenly jumped in the air and shouted loudly:" ... the hammer! Sledding! That's not what I imagined in my wildest dreams. "

The snowman was happy as never before. But Santa raised his index finger again and said admonishingly: "But watch out by the fireplaces! I've burnt my butt once before! "But the snowman let it go cold:" Oh,

I have so much snow, if I burn my butt, I'll just make a new one - haha. "Then he grinned at Santa , jumped on his sled and was gone.

And so the snowman saved Christmas, which was way too cold, but just right for the snowman!

NO DILIGENCE, NO PRICE

In the forest once lived a hamster and a squirrel. The hamster was always very diligent and did all his duties immediately. The squirrel, on the other hand, was very lazy. It would rather enjoy life; without all the annoying tasks that you had to do as a squirrel.

Every autumn, the animals began to gather supplies for hibernation. Squirrels, hamsters, mice and bears retreated to a cozy hideaway in winter to sleep a lot. Only when they got hungry did they wake up to eat. And there had to be something to eat.

So squirrels, hamsters, mice and bears gathered as much food as they could find and hid them in various places. In tree caves, empty bird nests, in the ground or even under stones. They collected more than they needed. Because it could be that other animals found the hidden food and - unknowingly - took the food of another. Or you forgot many a hiding place. That could happen - there were many.

So the hamster collected as much as he could. But the squirrel was lazy. He did not feel like collecting every day. It preferred to play by the stream or lay in the grass. When winter came, the squirrel realized that it was quite late and began to gather. Of course, time was not enough and the squirrel was very worried.

It asked the hamster if he would share. The hamster said, "You could have collected enough yourself! Why did not you do that? "The squirrel, however, had no excuse and replied," I had so much else to do. That's why I did not make it. Please, dear hamster, you have more than you need. Or should I starve to death? "

"All right," said the hamster, sharing his supplies with the squirrel. The squirrel was happy and thought, "Such a stupid hamster. That was easy. I'll do it again next year! "

When the next autumn came, the hamster again diligently collected food for hibernation. But what was that? The hamster saw the squirrel lying in the grass and dreaming. "What are you doing there? Why do not you collect anything? "Asked the hamster. The squirrel was startled, but again was not excused: "Did you scare me hamster. I'm just taking a break because I've collected so much, "it said.

When the winter came, the squirrel had not collected a nut, not a mushroom, not a cone or seed. With a single nut in his hands, the squirrel went to the hamster and said: "Come on, dear hamster, my whole food was stolen! Only this nut was left to me. What am I doing now? Surely you have more than you need, right? "The hamster shook his head." You have nothing? "He asked. The squirrel replied, "Not a nut, not a mushroom, not a cone or a seed."

The hamster said, "I did not find so much myself this year that it would do for two." The squirrel became angry: "You have not found enough for two? Why did not you say anything before? That's pretty mean of you hamster - do you know that? Had I known that, I would have collected myself! "

Then the hamster listened: "You have not collected?" The squirrel swallowed, when it noticed that it had revealed itself: "Well, well. I had a lot to do and then there was little time. "The hamster, however, now realized what he was talking to the squirrel:" That means you lied to me last year. And this year, you just wanted to make it easy for you. I understand that! "Said the hamster angrily.

"But do you really want to starve me?" Asked the squirrel. The hamster shook his head: "No, I will not let you starve to death. I'll give you enough that you do not starve. However, it will be too little to get full. I hope your growling stomach will open your eyes over the winter! "Said the hamster, giving the squirrel a small portion of his supplies.

The squirrel was angry with the hamster and did not seek the blame on himself. It thought, "This mean hamster. Had he told me early enough that he did not have that much, I could have collected something! That's all his fault! "Yes, the squirrel was so upset with himself that it was hard to admit that it had made a mistake.

However, the longer the squirrel was in hibernation and the stomach rumbled, the clearer it became to him that it was all to blame. It had to admit that it had made a mistake. Only then could the squirrel make it better for the next hibernation.

The next autumn, the squirrel gathered day one day. It ran quickly back and forth and collected more of everything. When winter came, the hamster went to apologize. The hamster was very happy about the squirrel's insight!

The squirrel offered the hamster some of his supplies as an excuse. But the hamster had enough supplies this year and said, "I was able to collect enough this year - thank you very much. But other animals may not have been so lucky. They would be very happy if you gave them some of your supplies. "

"That's how we do it!" Said the squirrel and gave some of his supplies to all the animals that did not have that much. The other animals were happy and thanked. But the squirrel said, "I never thought I would say that - but you can actually thank the hamster. He gave me a lesson that I will not forget all my life. "And so the animals thanked the squirrel and the hamster. Since then, all are the biggest friends and help each other - wherever they can!

GRANDPA HEINZ AND THE MERMAID

Tamara sits at the dining table with her grandparents - it's supper time. Grandpa Heinz once again tells the best stories. He used to be a sailor and experienced a lot. Granny Helene tells him over and over again he should not forget the food. But Grandpa Heinz is so in motion that he does not come to dinner.

He tells of sea monsters, mermaids and waves as tall as houses. "You're going to spin your sailor's yarn again!" Says Granny Helene. "This is not a sailor's yarn Leni!" Says Opa Heinz. "Listen to me for the first time." "Oh," grins Grandma Helene. "You only give the little boy a fuss."

After dinner, Grandpa Heinz proposes a walk on the beach. "Oh Heinz," says Granny Helene. "It's raining." But Grandpa Heinz is not deterred. "It almost stopped already. Plus, there's the right clothing for every weather, "he says, holding out the rain jacket to Tamara. "We'll be back in half an hour. Will you make us some hot tea? "He asks before Tamara and he walk out the door. And Granny Helene shakes her head and says what she always says: "You stubborn goat. Of course I'll make tea for you. You should not get any snuff. "

It is an uncomfortable weather. The sea is rough. But the rain has almost stopped. The rough sea reminds Grandpa Heinz of a stormy seafaring and he starts to talk. That's the beginning of a story that leaves Tamara quiet.

"I remember a seafaring trip that would hardly have survived your grandfather. It was a long time ago. I was still a young lad myself and did not go to sea much before long. The sea was even rougher than today and it stormed out of all the heavenly gates. The waves hit the cutter and the whole ship rocked back and forth. Some of the mariners were already afraid that the cutter would be full of water. So high hit the waves.

It was already dark and the rain whipped us in the face. In the dark we had lost sight and feared to walk on a sandbar keel. The best Kieker did not help you in the storm, you know? "Tamara looks questioningly at Opa Heinz:" Kieker? "" Yes, "says Opa Heinz. "This is a pair of binoculars. And before you ask, running a keel means the ship is stalling. "Tamara nods wide-eyed and with her mouth open.

Then Opa Heinz continues: "Eventually I did not even believe that we would arrive home safely. We did not even know which direction we needed to go. The storm continued to grow and I no longer saw the hand in my eyes.

Something suddenly shone in the water. At the light, I saw a little girl. Potz Blitz, I thought a stowaway had gone overboard and wanted to make my way to the bell. Then I saw the girl jump out of the water.

I could not believe my eyes. She jumped out of the water and into it again. Like a dolphin. But I tell you, that was not a dolphin. And it was not a little girl either. When I jumped out of the water, I recognized a huge fin. I'm sure that was actually a mermaid.

Again and again she jumped in the air and turned, until I understood that we should follow her. She swam ahead and shone the safe way into the harbor. This little mermaid has saved our lives! But then I never saw her again. Grandma Helene never believed me that. But it is the truth."

Tamara looks at Opa Heinz with an open mouth: "I believe you Grandpa. How did she look? "" Like a little girl. You could not see too much in the dark. I mean she had blond hair and a huge caudal fin. It was really fast - faster than any boat I knew by then. "

The rain has stopped and the sea has calmed down. A gentle breeze blows from the water and Tamara eagerly listens to every word that comes out of Grandpa Heinz's mouth.

What they do not know is that the little mermaid from Grandpa Heinz needs his help this time. And right now. Her name is Amelie. At that time, she told Grandpa Heinz the safe way to the harbor. Now she needs help herself.

Only a few hours ago she had been playing with the fish at the bottom of the lake. Then the sea freshened up and Amelie realized that she had swum farther out than she wanted.

For such a brave little mermaid that's not a problem you might think. But even for mermaids, the rough seas can be dangerous. Amelie swam toward the local cave vault, so she was not watching properly and a current seized her. She lost her footing and poked her head against a rock. Unconsciously, she was flushed to the beach and the tide set in.

It is the same beach where Grandpa Heinz and Tamara go for a walk. But the two are still too far away to help Amelie. However, a mermaid on land will not last long.

Amelie wakes up and realizes that she is ashore. The ebb has pushed the sea far back. She wriggles like a fish on the dry land, but she does not get on well. She could have done a short distance. But the sea is much too far away due to the ebb.

Discouraged, she gives up and bursts into tears. "Why does this happen to me? I've never done any harm. "She cries. "Oh darling, that has nothing to do with it." A voice suddenly says. Amelie swallows and wipes away her tears. But she sees nothing. "I'm up here," says the voice.

Now Amelie sees a little fairy with beautiful wings flapping over her. "What are you?" Asks Amelie. "Well, what does it look like? I am a fairy godmother. To be more specific - your fairy godmother. But you do not have much to do as a fairy of a mermaid, "she smiles.

"Fairies do not exist!" Says Amelie. "There are only in the fairy tale." The fairy looks confused Amelie: "Oh dear. And that comes just from a mermaid? You know that mermaids are as mythical as fairies? "

Amelie shakes her head: "No, there are many of us in the sea. We're not mythical creatures. "The fairy touches his head:" Oh honey, what are they teaching you down there? "Then she makes two fists and holds them against her hips:" No matter, important now is that we get you back into the water. And fast! "

"But how are you going to help me? You are far too small to take me back to the sea. "Amelie says disappointed and close to tears again. "Sweetheart," says the fairy. "That has nothing to do with the size. Even little ones can help! "

Then the fairy thinks: "Hm, how was the spell for a stranded mermaid? You have to apologize. I'm out of practice. Most of the time you're in the water and I'm ashore. How was that again? "

Then she swings her wand and murmurs a few words. The next moment the ground begins to fill with water under Amelie. The water becomes more and more, until Amelie is completely covered by water. The only problem is that the water is only around Amelie. She is swimming like a soap bubble now.

The fairy exhales sadly, "It was not that," she says. Then she raises an eyebrow and says, "But we have gained time. Technically speaking, once you are back in the water. "Amelie nods and is happy to feel water again.

But as much as the little fairy thinks, she does not come up with the spell. "It's getting pretty dark," she says. "I'll light up first." She waves her wand again and a small light floats next to her. "At least we can see something now."

A few meters further down the beach, go to Grandpa Heinz and Tamara. When Tamara discovers the light, she excitedly points to the glowing something: "Da grandpa. The light you have been talking about. "Opa Heinz scratches his head:" No, that's just a lantern. There's still someone who can walk. "" But it does not move at all. "Tamara exclaims excitedly. She pulls Grandpa Heinz's hand. "Come on Grandpa. This is your mermaid! "

Grandpa Heinz wonders if Granny Helene was right after all. Maybe he should not have told the story. Maybe he just puts Tamara in the head with it?

Suddenly he sees his mermaid floating on a beach in a bubble of water. He stands stiff as a stick: "What, but what?" He says, staring at Amelie. Tamara is quite outraged: "Da grandpa, you see? I told you. Is that the mermaid who saved you? "And Amelie recognizes Grandpa Heinz again. "You've gotten older," she says. "But I recognize you!"

Before the fairy could hear that, she's already flapping on Grandpa Heinz and boxing him with her little arms against his nose: "Stop!" She exclaims. "You will not touch Amelie, otherwise you will get to do it with me!" Grandpa Heinz carefully reaches for the fairy: "It's all right. I will do nothing to her. We know each other. "The fairy looks surprised Amelie over:" Is that true? "Amelie nods.

Grandpa Heinz comes closer to Amelie: "So your name is Amelie?" He asks. Then he points to Tamara. "This is my granddaughter Tamara." Amelie greets Tamara, who has now stopped babbling and standing with her mouth open. "You are beautiful!" Says Tamara and Amelie thanks.

Grandpa Heinz extends his hand to the water and says: "I could never thank you. You have saved my life! "At that moment, the fairy hits him on the hand:" Stay away from my water. "Then she waves her forefinger:" Touching the figure with the paws is forbidden. And now you go. We have work to do! "

DDThe fairy flutters to Amelie and tries hard to push the bubble of water. But she does not move. Amelie is too heavy. "I'll help you," says Opa Heinz and just wants to push with, as the fairy cries out: "NO! I said do not touch! "Grandpa Heinz stops jerking.

"If you touch the bubble of water, it will burst or worse!" The little fairy is just catching her breath as she sees little Tamara push the bubble of water out of the corner of her eye. "But how is that possible?" Asks the fairy.

Amelie nods to the fairy, "It's alright. Tamara is my soulmate. As I had felt with Heinz at that time, I feel it now with her. And I will eventually feel it with their children. "And Tamara pushes the little mermaid all the way back into the sea.

As Amelie is back in the sea, she jumps happily in the waves around. Then she shows up and waves to Tamara: "Thank you dear Tamara. We will definitely meet again! But now I have to go back, "she says, turning around and disappearing in the waves.

When Tamara turns around, the fairy is gone as well. Grandpa Heinz stands further back on the beach and beckons Tamara to himself. "Come on, little one, we have to go back, too. Granny Helene is already waiting for us with the tea. "

When they arrive at home Tamara tells how a waterfall. The story gushes out of her: "And then I pushed the mermaid back into the sea. She waved me once more and then disappeared. Even the fairy was gone then. "Granny Helene strokes her cheek:" Well, you have experienced a real adventure. But now the tea is drunk and then it goes into the trap. "

After Grandma Helene Tamara has gone to bed, she looks at Grandpa Heinz and smiles: "What did you do with her? She talked all the time until she fell asleep. The sailor's yarn that she spins does not fit any more. "Grandpa Heinz only smiles back and nods:" There's so much out there. And stories want to be told. Let her dream! "

Then grandma Helene and grandpa Heinz go to bed. And Grandpa Heinz is happy that he now has someone who believes in him and shares his stories with him. Even if it will remain a secret between the two. Tamara and he know there's a little mermaid out there called Amelie, who will always watch over them at sea.

THE HALLOWEEN NIGHT AND THE LITTLE VAMPIRE

High up on a hill stands an old house. The house is very run down because little Vladi and his family have been living here for a long time. It's exactly 200 years this Halloween. Yes, you heard right, little Vladi has lived here for 200 years, because Vladi is a vampire.

From the hill he can look over all the houses of the long winding road. Vladi sits at the window every day watching the kids. All year round - day out one day.

He observes them on their way to school, while playing and cycling, building snowmobiles and sledding - they laugh and rejoice. Some of the children have a lot of friends. Vladi does not have a single friend. At least no human. Only a spider and a cat keep him company.

Vladi would love to play with the other kids, but he can not. Not only that the other children are afraid of him, because Vladi is very pale and also has sharp teeth.

No, he can not. Because Vladi does not tolerate sunlight. It itches on the skin, that he wants to scratch constantly. And at night, when the sun is not shining, the other children lie in bed and sleep.

Vladi never sleeps. He does not have to, because he is a vampire. And vampires do not sleep. Oh dear, so Vladi has more time to get bored.

But once a year - for Halloween - Vladi sneaks out of the house. Because on Halloween, all children are on the streets at night and frighten each other happily. Disguised in spooky costumes, the children run around laughing. Since Vladi does not stand out. In this one night he walks around with the other children.

Tonight it is time again. It's Halloween. Vladi is very excited. In his cupboard he has hidden a small stuffed bag for the sweets. At nightfall he gets her out and storms to the door. One more look in the mirror - oh yes, that does not help. Vladi can not see himself in the mirror - that's the way it is with vampires. Of course it's hard to say, if you look good, too.

Vladi turns to his cat: "And Klara? How do I look? "The cat meows happily and strolls around his legs. "Perfect, I knew it," says Vladi. "I'm a pretty little vampire!" And then he shines all over his face before disappearing through the door into the night.

On the streets there is joyful bustle. So many kids in such great costumes. Then Vladi is suddenly stumped from behind: "Man, that's a blatant costume!" He hears a girl's voice. Vladi turns around. Behind him is a girl dressed as a witch.

"I did not manage my costume so much," she says, pulling on Vladis shirt. "That looks like it's already a million years old." Then she wants to grab Vladi's teeth: "Wow, they look really real." Vladi recoils and tries to step backwards. But his body is faster than his legs and so he plops on the butt.

"Sorry, I did not want that!" Says the girl, holding out her hand to Vladi. Vladi takes his hand and helps himself up. "But you have cold hands. Are you cold? "Asks the girl. Vladi quickly pulls his hand back and plops again on the butt. He had completely forgotten that. Vampires are much colder than other kids.

Vladi is quite confused. Something about the girl makes him rash and even clumsy. Normally he would never fall. He is way too fast for that. Because vampires are also much faster and stronger than other children.

"Why are you leaving?" Asks the girl. But Vladi does not answer. "Hm, you do not want to answer me?" She asks. But Vladi does not get a word out. He stands still and confused and looks at the girl with wide eyes.

As Vladi continues to make no sound, the girl pulls a pout and she looks at Vladi thoughtfully: "Hmm, well, then I'll start. I am Lana! But tonight I'm a witch, as you can see. "Lana turns around once to show her costume. Then she laughs shrilly and horribly: "Hi hi hi hi hi! Oh, that was a really good witch laughter. Now you! "Says Lana, thinks for a moment and then goes on:" I just noticed, I do not even know how a vampire laughs.

Since Vladi has to laugh: "Hu hu huuu." The laugh came out a little funny from Vladis mouth, that he is immediately embarrassed, that he laughed. "No!" Says Lana. "I do not think the vampires laugh like that. I think they laugh more like us. "

When Lana says so, Vladi looks at her again with wide eyes. He does not know what to answer. He can hardly say that he is a vampire and therefore vampires laugh just as he has just done. So he just smiles at Lana. At the same time his big teeth stick out in the corners of his mouth.

"That's a nice smile!" Says Lana. "You're right. Vampires are sure to smile sweetly. "Then she nudges Vladi, who becomes quite embarrassed:" Come on, you great vampire, let's collect sweets. "And so she pushes Vladi in front of her.

"Hey, I can walk myself." Says Vladi. "I believe you, but it is so much funnier!" Replies Lana and pushes on. Both run laughing through the streets. Vladi has never enjoyed collecting candies as much as she did with Lana. They are running from door to door and Vladi's bag is getting fuller. The adults love Vladi's costume so much that he always gets a little candy extra.

Arriving at the last house on the street, Lana says, "I have to go home!" That makes Vladi sad. "But we'll see each other tomorrow at school. You just have to tell me who you are. "

149

Vladi hesitates. Then he says, "Oh, I'm not from here, you know? We're just visiting for Halloween. "Now Lana is sad too. "That's a pity," she says. Vladi thinks. "But I'll be back next Halloween," he says, cheering Lana up. "Next year? That's really long, "says Lana. "But I'm glad we'll meet again." And she smiles at Vladi. Vladi smiles back - with his big teeth protruding from the corners of his mouth.

On the way home blows Vladi Trübsaal. A whole year is really long, he thinks. "So stupid," he mumbles to himself and kicks a stone away. The stone lands in front of a couple of big boys who are annoying a little boy in a clown costume. "I want to go home," says the little boy. But one of the big boys does not let him pass. "Before you go home, you leave us your sweets here," the big boy says with a nasty grin.

Well, that suits me right now, Vladi thinks. "Hey! Here you can have my sweets, "he says, offering his sweets to the big boy. Then he takes the little boy's hand and wants to bring him home.

The big boy, however, stands in his way. "Hey, wait a minute. Do you think, just because you give us your sweets, can the little one keep his own? I still want his. "Vladi looks at the big boy," Leave him his. You have mine. That must be enough. "Then he passes the big boy.

The big boy grabs Vladi's shoulder. Lightning fast, Vladi turns and grabs the big boy's arm. And so firmly that he can not move. Then he looks him in the eye - Vladi's eyes start to glow red. "I'll let you go now," says Vladi. As the big boys see the shining eyes, they get scared and run away.

But the little boy is totally excited about Vladi: "You're fast. How did you do this? I did not see how you move. And so strong. And the bright eyes. "

With big eyes there is a little boy in front of Vladi. In his eyes, Vladi can see the enthusiasm. "Yes," says Vladi. "I am fast and strong. But we will not tell anyone, ok? "

When Vladi looks up, Lana stands in front of him. Immediately he is pleased to see Lana. But then he notices that Lana has probably seen everything and he freezes. If he was not already so pale, he would be white now.

The little boy runs to her and falls into her arms: "Lana! Good that you are there. A couple of boys did not want to let me home. "Lana nods," Yes, Erik, I saw that. Are you alright? "She asks. The little boy shines and points to Vladi: "Yes, I'm fine. He chased away the bad guys. "Lana looks at Vladi:" Yes, he did. "Then she looks at Erik again:" Mom and Dad are looking for you everywhere. They're really sick of worry. "

Lana's little brother leaves his head sad. "Oh dear, now I'm sure I'll get in trouble." But then he stands straight up and says, "But the bad guys will never annoy me again." Lana almost laughs when she sees her little brother standing so proudly in front of him , Then she looks at Vladi: "This is my little brother. My parents are already looking for him. "

Vladi starts to stammer: "La Lana. I can explain that to you. "But Lana puts her index finger on her mouth. Then she looks down at Erik: "Hey Erik, are you going to go over there for a moment?" Lana points to a bench. Erik is not enthusiastic. But he still listens to his big sister. He goes to the bench, sits on it and rocks his legs.

Then Lana turns back to Vladi. For a short time there is icy silence. Lana just looks at Vladi but says nothing. Vladi is getting more and more restless. Then Lana gets air: "I ask you now what and you answer honestly, ok?" Vladi nods. "Are you ... are you a real vampire?"

Vladi hesitates and nods again. "But I do not do anything to anyone. These guys did not want to leave your brother home and ... "Lana interrupts Vladi:" It's alright, I believe you! "

Vladi looks at Lana: "Are you scared of me now?" Lana shakes her head: "Nonsense with sauce! I'm not scared. I think it's great! I really like vampires! I just always thought there are no real ones. And now

I'm meeting such a nice vampire like you! If I had not gone as a witch, I would have disguised myself as a vampire. "Lana hesitates," Oh, rubbish, what am I talking about, you're not disguised - I have to get used to that. " she smiles and continues, "I've never had such a great Halloween like today. And what you did for my brother is really great! "

Vladi looks at the floor. "Yes, but I lied to you. I'm from here. "Now he points to the house on the hill. "I live up there. And only for Halloween I go out. That's why I told you I was just coming for Halloween. Because otherwise the children sleep at night and during the day I can not get out because I can not tolerate the sun. "Now Lana smiles:" But that's great. "

Vladi is confused: "It's great that I can not tolerate the sun?" "No." Shakes Lana's head. "Not that." Lana hides her voice to act sternly, waving her index finger, "And not that you lied to me. That this never happens again to my little vampire. "Then she bumps Vladi in the side and both have to laugh. "But it's great that I can visit you every day now."

Vladi beaming all over his face: "You would do that?" Lana bends Vladi again in the side: "Of course. As much fun as we had today, we will have every day from now on. And you have to tell me everything about vampires. Are you doing that? "Vladi can hardly believe it. "Of course I do that!" And he shines again all over his face. And his big teeth are out again in the corners of his mouth.

Lana beams, too. "But now I have to bring my little brother home. My parents are already crazy with worry. "She says and gives Vladi a kiss on the cheek. That's when Vladi turns red for the first time in his life.

Immediately Erik points to Vladi and shouts: "Look Lana. It starts again. What he did before with his eyes. Now he does it with his whole head - look how red that is already. "And Lana laughs:" No Erik, come now. "She throws one last look at Vladi, who looks down and beckons bashfully.

Vladi walks happily home. Finally he has a girlfriend who plays with him all year round. That was the best Halloween for 200 years!

THE FEARLESS WILLBI

There used to be a little mouse in Africa. She lived in a small village on the edge of the jungle. In Africa it was very hot and in the village where the mouse lived there was no waterhole, no lake or even a small pond nearby. "Phew," the mouse snorted. "I have to get out of here." Said, done and so the mouse decided to visit her brother in the jungle.

There were many waterholes in the jungle. In her mind, the mouse was already swimming in the cool water and a smile crossed her face. "Brrrrr, the water is pretty cool." She thought. Quickly the bathing trunks packed into a small suitcase and off we went.

When she arrived in the jungle with her brother, the little mouse wondered about the house. All windows were tight and light was burning inside. The mouse knocked. Inside it rumbled and then it was quiet. The mouse knocked again: "Hey!" She called. "I heard you. Now get on Jonas! "The door opened a little gap. First there was a sniffing nose, then the blinking of small eyes.

Jonas threw open the door and jumped into his brother's arms, "Oh, Willbi. You are s. That's nice to see you. "Then Jonas looked around left and right. "Okay, come in quickly," he said and closed the door. Willbi looked around. Everything was pretty dark. "Why do you have the windows ... oh no," said Willbi. "I am here for a beach holiday! Nobody can handle the heat! So, grab your swimsuit and off you go! "

Jonas looked at Willbi anxiously, "You want to go swimming? To the water hole? But Willbi, that's where all the animals go. It's dangerous in the jungle! "" Excuse me? Pappalapapp, come on! "Jonas tugged on Willbi's arm:" No Willbi - really - it's too dangerous. So many animals are stronger than us and want to eat us. "But Willbi was not deterred. "If you do not pack your swimsuit, I'll do it!" He said, pulling Jonas after him.

The first thing they encountered was a lion. "Ahhh!" Yelled Jonas and scurried behind Willbi. Willbi looked at the lion. "What? Are you afraid of that? "Then he pulled his ears apart, stuck out his tongue, and made:" Bölölölölölöl. "But the lion just looked at him bored. "What?" Said Willbi. "You are not afraid of me?" The lion smiled tiredly: "I am the king of the jungle; why should I be afraid of a little mouse like you?"

"What, little mouse?" Said Willbi, pulling up his sleeves. "You're pretty naughty for such a hairy litter cat." Jonas tugged on Willbis shirt: "Listen to Willbi. He's much taller than us. "But Willbi waved his hand." Oh, pappalapap. People run away when I do that. Who really believes who he is? "

The lion looked at Willbi in amazement: "The people are afraid of you?" Willbi plumped proudly: "And whether! They jump on chairs and tables - if they see me! "The lion laughed loudly. Then he took a deep breath and yelled in the direction of the mice. Willbis ears fluttered in the wind of roar. It was so loud that all the birds nearby were startled and flying away.

But Willbi was unimpressed: "Pah, was that all? You should brush your teeth again! "Now the lion was startled. With a thoughtful look, he studied Willbi again. "You are not afraid of me? he asked. "Nope!" Willbi said firmly. "Why should I? You should be afraid of me! "

The lion did not really know what was happening. There was a small mouse with rolled-up sleeves in front of him, looking at him angrily. "You say: people are afraid of you? Prove it! "The lion finally said. "Pah." Willbi said. "No problem!"

They sneaked into the nearby village. The lion was afraid of humans and stopped more often the closer they came to the village. "What's wrong? Did the courage leave you? "Willbi called cheekily." "The little mouse really does not seem to be afraid," thought the lion.

When he arrived in the village, Willbi said: "Okay, Pussycat. You look through the window. I go in and show you how to deal with people. Jonas, you stay with the rental cat. "" What? "Jonas asked. "But he's eating me." "Oh, my," said Willbi. "The Mietze is not afraid of hunger." And went into the house.

The lion did not believe his eyes when he saw people jumping over tables and benches when they saw the little mouse. Willbi ran back and forth and made his face: "Bölölölölö". Then he came out again: "Na Mietzi? Now you, "he said. But the lion was too scared. And so they sneaked back into the jungle.

At the waterhole, Willbi jumped directly into the cool water: "Juhuuu!" - Splash - Other animals gathered around the waterhole when they saw the mice, but they did not dare, because the big lion stood there. Hyenas, Jackals, Wildcats ... everyone was waiting for their chance.

When the lion saw that, he just said, "Keep calm. Attack the mice - I will not stop you. "The hyenas were looking forward to a delicious snack. "But be warned," said the lion further. "I would not do it. These are the strongest mice I have ever seen. All humans have fled from them. I've watched it with my own eyes! "

The other animals were confused and looked questioningly at. A hyena lisped, "Alas, if the lion does not even eat it, I'll leave it." Another hyena stuttered back, "Well, there you are. If the lion d does not do that mmm ma, I will not do it either.

Willbi swam on his back through the waterhole and trumpeted: "What's going on? Just dare. You will experience your blue miracle! "But the animals slowly crept away. They were too scared of the mice - even people were afraid of them.

And even after Willbi had driven back to the village on the edge of the jungle, no one dared approach Jonas. He no longer hid himself, let in the bright sunlight through all the windows, and lived happily ever after.

THE STRANGE GIRL

One day a new girl came to kindergarten. Everybody thought her strange because she spoke only in rhymes. "Why are you talking so weird?" Little Marla asked the girl. The girl replied, "I'm not talking funny, that would be awesome. Almost astronomical and somehow stupid. "Then she went on. Marla stood with her mouth open: "Astro ... what?" She asked - but the girl was already out of earshot.

The more the girl spoke, the more children began to speak in rhymes. "Hello, kindergarten teacher, I have something in mind. I would like to have another tea. Would that be okay?"

The kindergarten teachers wondered about the children, who now only spoke in rhymes, but they also found it funny. And so they made themselves: "Hello dear children, we play a game now. The things of the inventor. Winning is the goal. "

It was not long before everyone in kindergarten spoke only in rhymes. When the parents picked up their children, they were very surprised that everything rhymed with what their children said: "We were almost only outside, I could barely catch my breath. It was so much fun. I did not think about the time. Now you are here and pick me up, can I still play short and sweet? "

The parents thought that was weird. Marla's mom asked Marla why she was talking so funny. Marla replied, "I'm not talking funny, that would be awesome. Almost astronomical and somehow stupid. "Marla's mom stood with her mouth open:" Astro ... what? "She asked - but Marla was already out of earshot.

The parents looked at each other in bewilderment. But then they began to rhyme themselves without realizing: "I see my child playing there. One among many. But it talks in rhymes. Will that stay that way? "Another mother turned around:" I can not say that, at least I do not believe it. But you too were talking in rhymes right now - almost like a poem. "Then everybody laughed.

Now a father intervened: "What should I tell my wife when she hears the child talking? I do not want to complain, but I'm a bit confused. "" You say that's normal - it's all rhyming now. If it were not so, then it would be fatal, because then it would be strange child. "

And so the parents began to rhyme. Then the parents' friends and it was not long before the whole country rhymed and those who did not rhyme were strange.

One day a strange girl came to kindergarten. It spoke without rhyming. Marla came and said: "You talk so funny. That's tremendous. Almost astronomical and somehow stupid. "

The strange girl asked in astonishment: "Astro ... what?" Marla looked at her: "I do not know what that means, but it sounds great," Marla said and shrugged her shoulders. Then the strange girl smiled and said, "I'm Luisa. Do you want to be my girlfriend, even if not everything rhymes what I say? "Marla thought for a moment. Then she took Luisa by the hand and said, "Sure! Let's play. I'll show you our great play area. "

And so the children gradually stopped rhyming. Then the kindergarten teachers stopped rhyming. Then the parents, the friends of the parents and soon the whole country.

And what do we learn from history? So it becomes strangely normal and normal becomes strange. But no matter how you are, it's as good as it is.

WHERE IS SHORTY?

The summer has broken out in the small village of Salbruck. Libby and her friends have long been waiting for the big heat wave to finally be able to bathe again at the Lasse quarry. Already in the morning the air smells of summer. Libby is on his way to Poppel to pick him up at school. Alex is coming too. At the corner of the Gaus-Alle Libby makes as usual a larger arc around the house of the old Bellbi. Old Bellbi has been living there for ages. At least he looks like this. Somehow the old man has something scary with all the wrinkles on his face and bony hands.

Libby and her friends once danced on Bellbi's property. Of course he caught her. Old Bellbi just gets it all. As if he had his eyes and ears everywhere. He chased the children from his property with his cane in hand. Since then, they have avoided the house.

Libby is driving past the house. Usually it is the same picture every morning. The old Bellbi stands on his lawn bleating and complaining to the neighbor, because his dog has allegedly done his business there again. The neighbor does not answer anymore. He takes his daughter to the car and pretends he does not hear Bellbi. That makes old Bellbi so mad that he gets louder.

The three friends have also seen how the old Bellbi complained loudly to his neighbor, because the dog had barked all night. He barely had an eye - heard the old man yelling. Whereby the dog of the Knigges really likes to bark at night. At least that's what Libby's mom says. She often protects old Bellbi and always tells how friendly he used to be when Mrs. Bellbi was still alive.

But today, nothing is to be seen or heard of old Bellbi. Also Mr. Knigge is not - as usual - in the driveway. Libby stops for a moment and scratches his head thoughtfully. "That's funny," she thinks. "Did something happen to old Bellbi?" She would like to check. But he does not dare and then he continues.

After a few minutes, Libby arrives at Poppel. Of course, Poppel is not his real name. Actually his name is Holger. But because he is a bit more stable, it looks kinda funny when he runs. At some point, Alex said: "Look, Holger comes running hoppeldipoppel." Alex and Libby had to laugh so hard that they called Holger from then only Poppel. By now he's so used to hearing Holger.

Alex is coming too. "Hey Alex - almost at the same time - what?" Libby shouts to Alex. Alex grins: 'Oh, Libby, did not even see you - yes, funny." Then the front door flies open and Poppel trumpets: "Well send her thick - everything in step?" That's Poppel's typical way. Always the big mouth in front path.

Libby shakes his head: "I think you'll never change Poppel!" Poppel beams over his ears: "But never my dear Libby - you sweetie!" He says and shakes Libby's hand. Libby has to laugh. But then she gets serious: "Hey guys, you know what I've been watching today? Old Bellbi was not complaining. "Poppel is closing his bike lock:" Oh, well, did he swallow himself or what? "Libby shakes his head:" No, seriously. He was not there. And Knigge was not in the driveway. I was thinking about looking to see if something had happened to the old Bellbi. "

Alex thinks: "Funny it is." But Poppel interferes immediately: "Nah no people, you can forget that right away. You probably do not remember how the old Zausel chased us off the grounds with a fat club. You can eat that nice. The thick one always gets it first! I can not get ten more horses! "Libby rolls her eyes:" Oh Poppel, you always have to overdo everything! That was a walking stick and not a club! "

Poppel waves down: "I do not care what you tell Libby. In my story that was a fat stick and I'll stick with it. "Alex shakes his head but then says," Either way, Poppel is right Libby. That brings nothing but trouble. In addition, we are slowly getting late. We should really go to school. If I'm late again, my dad turns right on the bike. "Libby nods and the three go.

The school day passes quickly and Libby does not mention the topic with the old Bellbi anymore. In the afternoon, the three friends drive to the Lasse quarry to test the water for temperature. Libby keeps his foot in the water and immediately winced. "Brrrr, is that still cold! The lake has probably not noticed the summer is. "Alex and Poppel laugh. Then Alex says, "We'll keep those few days off now. In addition, soon holidays. "Poppel nods:" Right! I am already counting the days. We have another week until the summer holidays. Then it will finally be donated again! Stop schoolwork and stuff! "

dThe next morning Libby drives her track as usual to pick up Poppel. But there is no sign of old Bellbi. Shortly before Poppel's house she sees Mr. Knigge, who is putting a leaflet on the fence. Libby stops to look at it. On the leaflet is a missing message for the dog of the Knigges. "That makes sense," she thinks. "If the King's dog ran away, then old Bellbi has no reason to complain."

Mr. Knigge sees Libby and approaches: "Hello Libby, Shorty disappeared the night before last night. While I have no hope that anyone will get in touch with the leaflets, if you see something, please call - yes? "Libby nods." Of course, Mr. Knigge, I'll do that for sure. "Libby had a summer last summer Watch out for the dog of the Knigges and has since gone to Shorty Gassi or played the dog sitter on weekends. Shorty has since become pretty fond of Libby.

Libby just wants to continue driving, as she stops again: "Mr. Knigge? It's a nice shock to me that Shorty ran away. I really hope they find him again. "Mr. Knigge turns around:" Many thanks Libby, but all the doors and windows were locked. I do not think he ran away. "Libby looks dumbfounded," Is that someone's kidnapping Shorty? "Mr. Knigge nods," It looks like it. "Libby is not sure what to answer:" That's it Yes unbelievable! Then I keep my eyes open in any case, "she says and goes on.

On the way to school Libby tells Alex and Poppel the whole story. Alex is horrified: "That's a strong piece! A dog hijack here in Salbruck? That's probably the most exciting thing that ever happened here, is it? "Libby agrees:" I agree. Do you think the old Bellbi has anything to do with it? "Alex shakes his head." Oh shit. He is at least 100 years old - how should he have anything to do with it? "Libby continues:" Just think, the old Bellbi has the biggest motive. He is constantly complaining about the dog. "

Poppel intervenes - somewhat out of breath from cycling - "Libby is right!" Poppel gasps: "I trust the old man too." Now he interrupts: "Hey guys, maybe we can stop, if we talk? I get gasp breathing! "The three friends stop and Poppel is breathing hard. "Ok, suppose old Bellbi had the faxes thick. What could be more appropriate than to make the dog disappear? "

Alex is not quite sure: "But how should he have done that?" Libby is very excited: "That's exactly what it needs to find out! We'll convict old Bellbi! "Poppel shakes his head." No, no, no, yesterday I did not make my point clear enough. I do not want to have anything to do with old Bellbi! "Libby looks at Poppel." Poppel, do not you want to pay the old man back? "

Poppel thinks for a moment. Then he answers: "Damn, yes, that sounds good. Then I play stick out of the bag! "Libby looks over to Alex:" Are you there too? "Alex hesitates, but then he agrees and extends his hand:" Oh, hell. Then the three musketeers are reunited. "Libby and Poppel put their hands on Alex's hand. Then all three cheer at the same time: "One for all and all for one!"

In the afternoon, the three hide in the bushes on the opposite side of the Bellbi House. Poppel has his binoculars for shading. "I did not know that so many people come by every day!" Says Alex. Libby says, "And we're not the only ones who suspect Bellbi," she says. "Did you see how they all shake their heads when they pass Bellbi's house?" Suddenly Poppel makes a cramped sound: "Ooh, have you seen that?

Lisa's mother just passed by and trampled on the flowerbed of old Bellbi. "

Alex reaches for the binoculars: "Show me! Fact, not a lie. Everything flat! Libby look. "Alex holds out the binoculars to Libby, but Libby does not take it. "What's going on?" Asks Alex. Libby looks thoughtful: "What if we do wrong to old Bellbi? If he was not? Everyone seems to think that old Bellbi has kidnapped the dog or worse. "

Poppel babbles immediately: "Are you kidding me Libby? And if that was the old stick vibrator! Anyone who goes after children, but before all animals has no respect! "Alex holds Poppel on the shoulder:" Wait Poppel. Libby is right! On television it is always - in doubt for the defendant. "Then he turns to Libby:" Listen to Libby. Even if he was not, we are his best chance of enlightenment. We're only here to find out the truth. "

Poppel puffs himself up: "To find out the truth? I think it hacks. I'm here to mop up the old Bellbi. "Alex shuts Poppel's mouth, still trying to keep talking," Hmmmmmmmmmmmmmmm. "Poppel frees his mouth," That's good. I understood. We're here to play Samaritan, for an old guy who did not deserve this. Alright Libby. I'm still here! After all, there is a chance that he is guilty and then I want to be there when the handcuffs click. "Alex looks at Libby:" All right Libby? "Libby nods:" All right! Let's find out the truth. "

Slowly dawn breaks and old Bellbi was not even visible. "Good that we told our parents that we're having an overnight party with you - Poppel," says Alex. "Class idea?" Replies Poppel. But Libby is not that enthusiastic: "Well, I did not think it was great to fool my parents." Poppel shakes his head: "Nonsense with sauce! We all spend the night together. What was lying there? "Alex looks at Libby:" Well, you have to admit, somehow that makes sense. "Libby nods:" That really makes sense. "Poppel interrupts the whole thing:" Pssst, well, rest now! It is dark! The mission begins. "

The three friends sneak across the street to the old Bellbi's fence. "Down Alex!" Hisses Poppel. "I can not go down. I'm just taller than you! "Libby intervenes:" Rest now you two or we'll fly up! "They sneak along the fence to the backyard. "Look," says Poppel. "An open window. Here we go. Avoid skid marks in underpants! "Then Poppel flits to the open window. "What's he doing there?" Asks Libby. "Was that the plan?" Alex shakes his head. "We did not have a plan. Come on! "Then he starts running too.

Poppel hangs on the window sill with his legs wriggling. "Now push one," he whispers. Alex tries to get his legs under control: "Shit, not so loud and stop fidgeting!" Suddenly Poppel stops fidgeting and stays still. "Did you hear that too?" He asks. Alex answers, "What's the matter?" And turns to Libby. Libby nods: "Yeah, I heard it too." Alex gets restless: "Yeah what? Is old Bellbi coming with a truncheon? "" No! "Whispers Poppel. "Then I would be over all mountains!" Libby looks around: "That was a soft barking. Well, as suppressed as a wuff. But that did not come from here. "

Alex pulls Poppel out of the window. "Boy, put that on my stomach." Poppel complains. "I really have to lose weight! But the noise came, I think, from across. "Alex is surprised:" Of the Knigges? Did the Shorty find again? "Libby pats Alex's forehead with the palm of his hand." Man, think about it, Alex! What would be the best way to show that the old Bellbi is not quite ticking anymore? The Knigges just pretended that Shorty was kidnapped. "Alex shakes his head," I do not believe it! "Libby nods to Alex," That's exactly what it is. Who would suspect that? Even I would not trust Mr. Knigge. "

Poppel is visibly disappointed: "Shit, and I wanted to wipe the old dry bean one. That will be nothing. But how can we prove now that the Knigges have only faked the kidnapping? "The three friends think. Then Alex says: "Helps nothing. Then we have to go in for the Knigges and convince ourselves. "Libby skin Alex again on the forehead:" Super idea Intelligence bolt. And then they put it down to kidnap and bring back Shorty. "Poppel has to stop laughing:" She's right, you're not the brightest chandelier in the chandelier, Alex. "Alex glares at Poppel:" Ha ha, very funny dickers. "Libby walks between the two:" Now stop! I have an idea."

After half an hour you hear police sirens approaching the House of the Knigges. Two patrol cars and a police car stop in front of the house. A handful of police rush to the door. Just as they want to break open the door, it swings open and Mr. Knigge stands in the doorway. "What's happening? So much police for a dog hijacking? Did you find Shorty? "

The policeman looks surprised: "We have received a call from her daughter that the abductor is now in the house." Mr. Knigge shakes his head: "That's nonsense. My daughter is sleeping soundly. "But the policeman persists:" Mr. Knigge, please step aside. We need to be sure. "Mr. Knigge stops in the doorway," And I tell them - they will not search my house. "Two police officers take Mr. Knigge aside and the rest of the forces search the house.

When the police come out, one of the officers wears Shorty in his arms. "Um, Mr. Knigge, will you explain that to me please?" Mr. Knigge reaches for the dog: "Yes, I did not mention that, Shorty was brought back. Thank God! "The policeman takes a step back and keeps the dog in his arms. "When we arrived, they asked if we had found their dog. In addition, her daughter actually slept and can not have called accordingly to the police. We must now clarify this situation. "

At this moment, Libby, Alex and Poppel are brought to the front door of the Knigge by one of the other policemen. "And who are you?" Asks the policeman with the dog in his arms. Libby tells the whole story and apologizes for lying on the phone. The policeman bends down to her. "All right, little lady. As Chief Inspector, I tell you, you've done just the thing - calling the police. It would have been better, however, to tell the truth. "Then the commissioner smiles:" On the other side, not everything was lying. "And looks at Mr. Knigge. "The dog hijacker was really in the house. Is that right, Herr Knigge? "

When the Commissioner addresses Mr Knigge directly, it breaks out of him: "I only did that because I was desperate. Every day the bleating of old Bellbi. I could not stand it anymore. "The commissioner nods:" All right, Mr. Knigge, but there are definitely other ways. Please accompany us to the guard now. "Two policemen bring Mr. Knigge to the patrol car.

Then the inspector looks again at Libby, Alex and Poppel: "And now we bring you three home better." Poppel shakes his head and waves: "No, not necessary. I'll go alone. See you guys! "But the commissioner stops him:" Do not worry my boy. You are almost heroes. Your parents will be proud of you. But we still need your statements and that's best done together with your parents. And after that you should go to bed too, right? "

Poppel shines all over his face: "Heroes? Yes, I want to be a hero. I always knew that. It's time for my parents to find out about it and the school and the city ... "While Poppel is still chattering, the three are taken to the patrol car.

Libby is still stunned that Mr. Knigge himself was the dog hijacker: "It's hard to believe that Mr. Knigge was himself. I can not believe it, "says Libby. Poppel grins and pulls Alex up. "Yes, Alex, tell me that as the brightest light in the chandelier - can you believe it?" He sneers. Alex snappily answers: "Not everyone can be such a great hero as you hoppeldipoppel!" And everyone laughs.

HEINRICH THE COCK CAUSES UPROAR

Not so long ago a cockerel lived on a farm and his name was Heinrich. Heinrich had many friends. Although he liked to stroll around the yard with a cocky attitude and never listened carefully, the animals knew that Heinrich was a nice cock at heart. He had the donkey, the dog, the pig, the cow, the sheep and the horse as a friend. Every day they played catch and many other fun games.

But one day Heinrich heard the farmer say to his wife: "Do not forget to make the cake tomorrow." "Which cake?" Asked the woman. "Well, Henry should roast!" Replied the farmer. Heinrich was scared and afraid. "I should be fried? I'm too pretty for that! "He thought and sneaked away.

He called all friends and told him what he had heard. The horse shook his head. "No," said it. "I can not imagine that." But Heinrich stuck to it: "I heard it with my own ears!" He said. "And that should be celebrated with a cake?" Asked the donkey. Heinrich was furious: "Well, if I tell you!" "Oh dear, what should we do?" Asked the cow. "We save Henry!" Said the dog determined.

So the animals made a plan. The dog chased the sheep with a loud barking and distracted the farmer. The donkey opened a kitchen window over the stove. The horse leaned through the window and pulled the hose off the stove with a strong bite. Heinrich, the pig, and the cow stood dope. Without the hose, the stove did not work. And if the stove did not work, no one could be fried either.

But the farmer noticed the broken hearth and set about repairing it. When the animals saw that, they were disappointed. "That did not work!" Bleated the sheep. But the dog remained determined: "We can do it. Then another plan has to come! But we must not attract attention now, "he said. The animals nodded and sneaked into their orders.

As night fell, the animals met in the big stable to make a new plan. The pig already had an idea: "When my feeding trough was broken once," said it, "I had to wait for a new trough until I got something to eat."

"That's smart!" Said the dog. "If there are no pots and pans, nothing can be fried." The horse nodded, "Why did not we think about it soon?" It asked. "Good things take a while," said the cow. But Heinrich did not look as if he had "while": "Good things take a while?" He asked. "We are running out of time! Now break with time and a bit more hurry - but zz! "And he ran.

The other animals looked after him in puzzlement. When Heinrich noticed this, he stopped: "Come on, people! What's going on? "The donkey asked sheepishly," What is ZZ? "Heinrich hung his head and took a deep breath:" That means: pretty fast. Can we do it now? Yes?"

When the donkey heard that, he turned to the animals and began to laugh: "Ah, ah, oh well, pretty quickly. That's funny. "When the animals heard the donkey laugh, they also laughed. And everyone laughed heartily together. All except Heinrich. He stood behind the donkey waving his wings wildly: "Hello! That's not funny either! It's time! "The dog nodded laughing and said," Yes, but the donkey really looks like Henry! "" Yeah, nice! It's all about my plumage and not about your fur, "Heinrich grumbled. The dog nodded again and said: "Yes, you are right! "Yes, you nod, but the clock is ticking!" Answered Heinrich. And so the animals sneaked back to the farmhouse.

The donkey opened the door. The dog went in first. The pig, the sheep, the cow and the horse formed a chain outside to the stable. So they started to hand out all the pots and pans from the farmhouse to the stable. At the end of the chain Heinrich dashed to hide all the pots and pans in the straw.

In the house it suddenly popped "PENG". Heinrich was shocked: "What was that?" At the very front, there was a whisper: "Nu in Pfn run fan." Heinrich understood only half and became more and more nervous: "What is that? What's happening? The dog told it to the donkey, the donkey to the pig, the pig to the sheep, the sheep to the cow and the cow to the horse - until the quiet post arrived at Heinrich: "Just a pan fell down."

"What?" Cried Heinrich. "And the farmer? Did he wake up? "And again the silent post went off. From the horse to the cow, from the cow to the sheep, from the sheep to the pig, from the pig to the donkey and from the donkey to the dog. The dog answered and Heinrich again understood only half. "Nn st al ru." And so the answer went from the dog to the donkey, from the donkey to the pig, from the pig to the sheep, from the sheep to the cow, from the cow to the horse and the horse told Heinrich: "No, that's all calm. "the horse finally said. Heinrich was relieved.

The next day the farmer came to the stable and all the animals were restless. They all mixed up. Behind the farmer came the farmer's wife with a huge cake in her hands. "The cake here? For what? "Asked the cow. "Should she be one of us?" The pig asked. "For what reason?" Asked the dog. Then suddenly Heinrich remembered that he has his birthday.

Of all the confused talk of animals, every other human being would only hear, "Wuff Mash Grunz Muh." The farmer watched the animals and did not want to disturb. He knew his animals and knew what they were waiting for: "Relax now, please! Heinrich should guess! "

Then Heinrich fell like scales from the eyes. The farmer did not say he should fry. He said: "he should guess." Heinrich was relieved and everyone was happy that Heinrich had simply not listened properly.

The animals celebrated Heinrich's birthday and were happy. The farmer sat with momentum in the straw. "Well, what's so hard here?"

The farmer asked indignantly. But the animals celebrated and acted as if they had heard nothing

And what do we learn from the story here? Proper listening is very important for humans and animals!

WHERE IS MOM DUCK?

At a large pond, surrounded by greenery, Mama Duck is just in her nest and is very proud as the offspring hatches from the eggs. The little ducks break the shells and stick their little heads out. Then they wiggle their butts and shake the remaining shell from the bottom.

Mommy Duck affectionately sticks her beak in greeting each one of them. The little ones know immediately that this is the mom. Then Mama jumps into the water and one after the other jumps behind. They swim in a line across the pond - the proud mom in front away.

But, oh dear, what is that? A chick has not hatched yet. It rumbles and rolls in the nest criss-cross. With a lot of momentum it falls on the meadow and the egg breaks on a stone. The egg shell flies around and the little duckling shakes a lot. Carefully, it looks around. No, nobody is there. Hm, funny. So the duckling waddles to look for his mom.

After a short time the duckling meets a frog. The frog sits on a branch by the water and quacks. "Hurray!" Thinks the duckling. "That must be Mama." It runs to the frog and quacks happily with. The frog looks at the duckling: "What are you doing here?" Asks the frog. The duckling answers: "I quake with you, mamma!" The frog shakes his head: "I'm not your mom!" He says and jumps off.

The duckling is sad. Thought it did find his mom. With hanging head it waddles on. After a few steps, it encounters a bird. The bird chirps happily to himself. The duckling looks at the bird and thinks, "This is not a croak, but it has feathers. Maybe that's my mom. "And then it sits next to the bird and quacks loudly. The bird is outraged: "Why are you covering my beautiful song with your gequake?" He asks. Then he picks the duckling upside down and flies away.

Now the duckling is really sad and tears are rolling down his cheeks. "I will never find my mom again!" It quietly sobbing to himself. There comes a fox to the duckling. "Well little duckling, why are you so sad?" Asks the fox. "I am looking for my mom. I'm all alone! "Says the duckling. The fox grins insidiously and says, "Come with me. Together we will find your mom. "

The duckling is happy: "Hurray!" And runs after the fox. After some time, the duckling asks the fox, "How long are we going to walk? We are almost in the forest. "The fox answers:" Do not worry. Your mom is there waiting for you. "

The fox does not have to find the mum. He wants to lure the duckling into the forest to eat it in the shelter of the trees. The fox grins and thinks: "That's too easy. I do not even have to wear the duckling, it goes by itself into the forest. "

Arrived at the edge of the forest, the duckling stops: "It is dark there in the forest!" Says it anxiously. "You do not have to be scared!" Says the fox. "I've hidden your mom there to keep her safe. "Sure, what?" Asks the duckling. The Fox answers in a worried voice, "You know, there are many evil animals that would love to eat you. But do not be afraid, I'm not one of them! "

Just as they wanted to move on, a bear stood in the way: "Na fox? Where do you want to go with the duckling? "He asks. The fox ducks in shock: "Hello big bear, where do you come from so suddenly? I only help the duckling to find his mom! "The bear looks at the duckling. Then he asks in a growl voice: "Is that the little duckling?" The duckling jumps up and down: "Yes! The fox hid them in the forest because there are so many evil animals. "

The bear immediately suspects what the fox is up to. "So so. So there are many evil animals here. "He growls. Then he looks at the fox suspiciously: "Well, luckily you are not one of them, Fuchs. Right? "The fox shakes his head quickly:" No, no, but of course not. I just wanted to help the poor duckling. "The bear takes the duckling protectively into his paws and says," Well, that's great that the fox has helped you so far. Now I'll do better. Your mom is not in the woods any more. I think she went to the pond to look for you. She misses you very much, you know. "Then he looks again at the fox and asks with a threatening look:" Is it true Fox? "The fox nods quickly with his head:" Yes, yes, now that you say it falls give it to me again. She walked to the pond earlier. "Then the fox looks at the duckling:" Your mom is back at the pond. I completely forgot that, yes. "

So the bear takes the duckling. On the way to the pond, the two meet the bird. The duckling trembles. "What do you have?" Asks the bear. The duckling ducks and whispers: "The bird picked me because I thought it was my mom." The bear looks at the bird and grunts: "Look here in your face, the duckling probably speaks the truth. It's also your duty to help, but you did not help the poor duckling! "Then he takes a deep breath:" We'll talk about that when I get back, "he says and carries on the duckling. The bird flutters off quickly.

Next, the two meet the frog. The bear looks at the duckling: "Did the frog also do something to you?" The duckling answers: "No, he just jumped away." The bear looks at the frog angrily and growls: "Here I look into your face, the duckling probably the truth speaks. It's also your duty to help, but you did not help the poor duckling! "Then he takes a deep breath:" We'll talk about that when I get back, "he says and carries on the duckling. The frog hops off quickly.

When the two arrive at the pond, the duckling is happy, as it sees the mom. It cheers and jumps headlong into the pond: "Thank you bear! call it to the bear. "And thank you also to the fox of mine." The bear growls loudly backwards: "You're welcome to play little duckling. And do not worry, I'll certainly thank the fox powerfully. "

When the fox hears this, he pricks his ears in alarm. "Oh my, now it's still my collar," he thinks and runs as fast as he can over all the mountains. Since then, the fox has never been seen again. The bear, however, still keeps a watchful eye on the little duckling, so that never again a clever fox comes to stupid thoughts.

MOM GETS A BABY

Mom and Dad were very excited today when they got home. Grandma knew immediately what was going on. It all felt very strange to me. Grandma squeezed Mama all the time and then passed her hand over Mama's stomach. Sometimes she hugged mom and dad at the same time. As with group cuddling in kindergarten. But when the group cuddles nobody cries. Grandma was crying all the time. "Why are you crying?" I asked. Granny raised her glasses and wiped her tears away: "These are tears of joy my little sparrow," she said. Then she hugged me and squeezed me tight. She said again and again: "Oh my little sparrow." Then Mama leaned down to me and said: "Tobias, you get a sibling."

So that's it. That's why everyone was so excited. Now I was really excited. "I'm getting a little brother!" I called. But mom said, "You get a sibling my sparrow. Maybe it's also a little sister. "I thought for a moment. A little sister? What should I do with it? Then I said firmly, "I'd rather have a little brother. Girls are stupid. "And everybody laughed.

The next day in the kindergarten, I proudly told that I'm getting a little brother. Our kindergarten teacher, Mrs. Aalfeld, asked me if mom and dad already knew what it would be like. I did not understand the question. But then she explained it to me. She said if mom and dad already knew that I would get a brother and not a sister. "Yes!" I said. "I told Mama I want a brother." Ms. Aalfeld then said that I could not decide that easily because it was just coincidence what you get. I did not lose my head all day.

My friend Fabian later told me that this is like Christmas presents. Before you do not know what you get. Only when you unpack the gifts.

"But that's exactly why I told Mama what I want," I told Fabian. "Does not that go with the wishes of Santa Claus?"

"Yes," said Fabian. "It works the same way." And Fabian had to know, because he became a big brother last year. "But you still get something different sometimes," he continued. "You do not always get what you wanted." Now I was not so happy anymore. I thought about what it would be like to have a little sister. What should I play with? Girls always play such stupid things. But then I remembered that Mama said, if it does not fit, we can exchange it.

At home, I watched Mama cooking. "Mom?" I asked. "When do I get my brother?" Mom laughed: "Sparrow, you mean your sibling. If everything goes as planned - probably right at Christmas. Would not that be a great Christmas present? "

And there it was - Christmas. So Fabian was right. It will be a Christmas present. That means: Mama can exchange it. Suddenly, I had another very different question: "Do I also get other things for Christmas?" My mom choked with laughter. What was so funny again? Somehow I did not understand all that. "Sparrow, you get other presents for Christmas. Your sibling is a very special Christmas surprise. "Then she took another sip of her water.

Good, that was clear. Then now to exchange: "So, if I should get a sister, you can exchange it for a brother, right?" Suddenly, Mama snorted all the water out of her mouth. "You got me cold," she laughed, wiping the water from the table. "Sparrow, no matter if you get a brother or a sister, you'll love your sibling very much. And your sibling will love you very much and look up to you because you are the big brother.

Do you know what - looking up to you - means? "I shook my head. "Your sibling will be very proud because it has such a great big brother. Just as you look up to Spiderman. "Now I knew what Mama meant. I'm a superhero for my sibling! "I'll always protect my sibling,"

I said, making my Spiderman move. "Do, do ... do, do ... there are the nets flying," I called. And I was already on my way to my nursery. I had to prepare.

But before I could make any preparations, it was already bed time. "Mom, I'm not finished yet," I said as I brushed my teeth. But Mama said I had enough time until Christmas and she was right.

We had a lot of fun during the summer. Dad often said mom should not work so hard. That would not be good, because she carries my sibling in her. I tried to imagine that; but somehow I found that pretty weird. I used to hear very different things about how babies are born. From stork to rainbow there were great stories. But Fabian explained to me: "The child grows in the mother's stomach," he said. "When it's old enough, it's taken out by a doctor and cleaned up. Not because Mama is dirty in the stomach, but because the baby is swimming in the water from a fruit. "I looked at Fabian," Like banana juice? "I asked. "Exactly. Something like banana juice. Tastes delicious and is healthy. But it sticks very well when you use it "That sounded strange to me, but it seemed to be true. After all, Fabian had to know it. And Mama's stomach became rounder, too.

The bigger the belly became, the less mom could do with me. I thought that was stupid. But dad told me that's normal and that I should help mom - wherever possible. And above all, I should be good. Because the mom should not be upset. As if you had to tell me that. "Child's play," I said. "Grandma says I'm always nice."

So I helped Mom wherever I could. If I brought Mama what she needed right away, she thanked me and gave me a peck. I felt really grown up. If dad was not there, I was the man in the house now. Nevertheless, I was allowed to play and romp. Otherwise I would not have wanted to be the man in the house - adults always do so boring things.

In the fall it was more and more about the baby, even though it was not there yet. Mom and Dad kept getting stuff for the baby. Whenever we had visitors, everyone just talked about it. Dad had even less time because he was preparing the nursery - painting, building furniture and stuff like that. Whenever I wanted to play something, he always said, "Later my sparrow. Let Dad just finish it. "But then it was too late or Dad was broken and had to rest. I was pretty bored.

I started to wonder if that will be the case when the baby is there. That would be completely stupid. But as always Fabian Rat knew: "That's just the beginning," he said. "Because the baby does not sleep long and Mom and Dad often have to get up at night. Then they are tired during the day. But that stops. In between, they have a bad conscience. That's what my grandma says. That means they're sorry they do not have that much time for you right now. Then you often get a gift, or an ice cream, or may television. It's actually quite cool. "As Fabian told me, that sounded quite good and I was looking forward to my sibling again.

It came the Christmas Eve and everyone was looking forward to the baby. But my sibling was quite time. Mom and dad still had not told me if it would be a brother or a sister. Although the grandma thought that they already knew. I think that means I get a little sister. But I do not care about that now. With a sister I could give tea parties or play coffee and cake. I could not do that with a brother. That would be funny.

Anyway, we have Christmas Eve now and the whole family is in the hospital. Slowly I am getting tired and I have not yet unpacked a present. Grandma says we'll do it tomorrow morning. But I want to unpack gifts today. So I bravely open my eyes and stare at the clock. The small and the big hands are pointing upwards. That's really late. Suddenly dad comes running up and shouts: "He is alive and kicking!" Immediately everyone jumps up and is happy. I'm of course the loudest. At least we manage to unpack presents. But wait a minute, Daddy said. So I got a little brother after all. I would not have had to worry about that because of the exchange. Grandma presses me tight and says, "Merry Christmas my sparrow. There you have your first present. A little brother. "

The whole family follows Dad down the hall to a large window. There are a lot of babies behind it. But dad says: my little brother is not there right now. So everyone goes on to a room where Mama is. I immediately run to her and cuddle my head to her arm. "All right, my sparrow. Mom is doing great, "she says, stroking my hair. Suddenly a nurse comes in, holding something in her arms. She gives mom my new little brother, who is a lot smaller than I thought.

"May I introduce you?" Mom says. "That's David, your new little brother." "He's really small!" I say, as my grandmother bites me from behind: "Well, let's go home and unpack presents?" I shake my head: "Oh Do you know, Grandma, that has time until tomorrow. David needs his big brother for the first time. "She presses me tight and Dad says:" Look at how grown-up you are already. You'll be a great big brother! "" Yes! "I say. "And now he needs rest and mom too."

Daddy lifts me up on the bed and says, "You are right! Then watch out for the two of them. "When he lets me go, I cuddle up to Mama and David. "Then we'll let you rest for a while." Papa says before he pushes everyone out of the room.

Besides Mama, it is totally comfortable and I notice, how I am getting tired. "Well my sparrow," Mom whispers. "So you have a little brother now. As you wished. "I have to yawn. "Uh, oh Mama, I would have been happy about a little sister, too" I say and fall asleep on Mama's arm.

LARIS AND LORAN

In space, two little males fly through space in a spaceship. At the wheel sits Laris and Loran sits in the passenger seat as a co-pilot. The two are a fun team. Laris is always very grumpy and quickly annoyed. Loran, on the other hand, is very timid and babbles like a waterfall. The two get into the strangest situations. But see for yourself...

The spaceship is not far away from the earth, when suddenly red lights come on and a signal sounds: "Beep, beep, beep." "Did you forget to refuel Laris?" Loran asks Laris is annoyed: "That sounds again like a reproach. You could have even thought of it! "Loran grips Laris hectic at the space suit:" So you forgot to refuel! "Laris is shaken back and forth:" You forgot to refuel! By the great Davin, that was my beautiful life. Oh, you beautiful universe, how will I miss you. "

Laris looks annoyed at Loran: "Is that it? Are you done? "Loran puts the back of his hand on his forehead. Then he says in a whiny voice: "No, not yet. I say goodbye to the sparkling stars. You have always shone so bright in the hours of my distress. And the planets on which ... "Laris interrupts Loran:" The next planet is Earth. There we get fuel and then we fly on. "Loran opens his eyes:" There is a planet nearby? Oh Davin, thank you! Dear stars, dear planets, I will stay with you. "

Then Loran suddenly stops: "Oh, oh, you want to land there, right? Who lives in this planet? Oh, by the big Davin, we're going to die! "Laris tears the thread of patience:" Now settle down. But you're also a coward! "Then he taps around on a small device and begins to read:" On Earth live humans and animals. Where humans are the more advanced form of life. It says here that they can make their own decisions. That sounds good - they can certainly help us! "

Said, done, Laris is heading for Earth. Loran is still restless: "And what are animals? Can they think too? Can they also make decisions? Can

they, can they ... "Loran suddenly sticks to the windowpane:" Uiiii !!!
That looks nice. That's so blue and so green and so friendly. Is that the
earth? "The spaceship approaches a large blue-green sphere. "No,
that's a coconut. Of course that's the earth. What else is that supposed
to be? "

Loran crosses his arms. "You do not always have to be so mean, Laris.
Is fuel still enough to land? "Laris makes a thoughtful face:" According
to my calculations, we are missing a few drops. But what are a few
drops? We'll pack that for just 15 minutes until the impact! "Loran
looks at Laris, aghast:" What are some drops? Are you serious? Oh the
big Davin, he said impact. We will crash on the earth. "Laris hisses
Loran:" But that's enough! Do not get into the spacesuit right away.
Put on the seat belts and think of the flaps! "Loran is outraged:" That's
what concerns you now? The flaps? Incidentally, I forgot that only
once. Once only!"

After 15 minutes, the time has come. Laris and Loran make a crash
landing in a small shrubbery. It bangs and rumbles. Then it rustles.
From the bushes you can hear Loran: "What is that strange noise? Do
you hear that, too, Laris? As if someone sniffs loudly. Laris, I'm talking
to you. Do you hear the? Laris! "Loran slumps out of the bushes right
in front of a dog.

"Oh, my goodness!" Loran sees in front of him a dog juggling a football
on his head and whose huge dog's snout is almost as big as him.
"LARIS !!!" Laris jumps out of the bushes. Loran looks at him: "Is this
a human? But they are pretty hairy! And the fashion here is cruel!
What is this funny black and white ball on the head? All right, what
the hell. "Loran clears his throat:" Hello man. We come in peace. "Laris
shakes his head:" Loran, this is not a human. That's an animal! "

Loran stops completely: "An animal? And now? "Laris whispers:" No
fast movements now! Animals can be dangerous. "Loran swallows:" D
... d ... you tell me now? "Suddenly a loud whistle sounds. Loran winces
and closes his eyes. "Oh, by the big Davin, that's it!" But the dog turns

and runs away barking. Laris wipes his forehead: "Phew, that was close. I am relieved."

Loran winks with one eye and sees now that the dog is gone. Then he begins to complain: "You are relieved Laris? For real? Are you relieved? "But Laris waves off:" Oh calm down Loran, nothing happened. Come on, come on! We are looking for a human and then we can finally disappear again. "Loran follows Laris and does not stop chattering:" Oh, calm down Loran. Nothing happened. As if always something had to happen first. That's a joke, Laris. I got away just then. But the big Laris says: Calm down, Loran, nothing happened ... "And so Loran talks without a dot and a comma, while Laris covers his ears.

Suddenly the huge black-and-white ball hat gets shot and gets Loran Loran kills with the ball down the slope. Laris notices that the bitching has stopped and turns around. There he sees Loran rolling down the hill with that weird big thing. "Oh, the big Davin. Loran, hold on. I'm coming! "Laris runs after the ball hat. Loran rolls straight towards a lake. At the last moment, the comic hat of Loran dissolves and he stays on the edge of the lake. Laris is also here: "Loran, can you hear me? How are you? "Loran's eyes are jumbled all over each other:" Hey Laris. You brought your twin brothers. I did not even know you had any, "Loran grins before fainting.

When Loran wakes up, Laris sits beside him: "Na Loran, are you alright? Is it going again? "Loran looks around:" Where am I? What happened? "Laris reminds Loran of the incident with the weird thing. Loran immediately jumps up: "Oh, yes, we are on earth. By Davin, we have to get out of here! What will happen next? It's dangerously here on this planet. "Laris grins. "Why are you grinning like that? Do you think that's funny? "Laris shakes his head." No, Loran. Look around. "

Loran looks around and sees the lake. Eyes wide and open-mouthed, he stands amazed on the shore: "That's ... that's ..." Laris ends his sentence: "Right, that's a lot of fuel!" Loran makes aerial leaps: "Juhuu.

Thank you Davin. We did it! "Laris jumps in:" Yes, we did it! And with the quantities we can always bring fuel here! "Loran stops jumping:" What? Are you still in comfort? Again and again? I'll never set foot on this planet again. Do you actually know what happened to me here? I'll remind you. So. When we arrived here ... "Laris shakes his head and gets enough fuel for the onward flight while Loran chatters and babbles ...

So the two fly on and have a great story to tell again. And if you see a bright spot moving in the sky at night, that's probably Laris and Loran. Then you might even hear Loran chattering.

The Door

Once upon a time there was a woman who had two children. A boy and a girl. One day she went on the journey and said to them, "Listen, children, I am leaving and you are staying home alone. That's why it's a good fit for the rear door. " She meant that they should be careful that no thief creeps in through the rear door.

She had been gone a while, when the two got bored, and the brother said to the nurse: "Come on, we want to go out into the forest a little bit, and we'll take the rear door, then it's good!"

She was satisfied and they went out into the woods. But as they ran around, they got lost and the night overtook them, so they saw that they would not be coming home, and with fear they climbed on an oak tree to stay there until morning so they would not be aware of the wild beasts torn up.

For a while they sat there, thieves came and hauled in a lot of money, they want to count. Since the little ones keep very quiet in the tree, so they are not noticed by the men.

But at last his brother can not keep calm anymore and he says to his sister: "I have to do something small."

"Well, do it!"

There he does it, but the thieves quietly continue their money and say, "It's a little rain falling."

Again after a while the brother says to the sister: "I can not hold it any longer, I have to do something big."

"Well, then do it!"

There he does it, but the thieves quietly continue to count and say, "It's a little crap of the birds sitting in the tree."

Now they sit quietly for a long time, when suddenly the brother says: "I can not hold the rear door anymore."

"So throw her down!" Says the sister.

Then he throws her down and she falls in the midst of the thieves, and they hurry away and shout: "The clouds are falling from the sky, the clouds are falling from the sky!"

Now it was almost morning, and then brother and sister went down from the tree, and took the rear door and the money the thieves had left, and returned home happily.

The mother went to meet them and whined and scolded that they had not taken care of the rear door and now thieves had been there and took everything.

The little ones, however, told everything as they had done in the forest, and there she was glad. And with the money she bought new clothes and new equipment, and there was so much left over that they all had enough of it all their lives.

Wise Owl

Long ago, an owl lived deep in the forest. She nestled in the mighty crown of an oak and listened gladly when the animals of the forest told of their joys and sorrows.

Even the owl liked to tell stories that the wind and the rain had brought her from far away. One day, however, she decided to leave the deep forest and move out to hear new stories.

She spread her wings and flew into the wide world. With her big eyes she saw everything, everything she heard with her sharp ears, and everything kept them carefully in her memory.

So the years went by and the owl got older and wiser. Then she longed for her forest and the big oak tree and she decided to go home.

She flew for many days and nights, until she was silent in the crown of the old Eichelandete.

When the animals of the forest heard that the wise owl had returned, they gathered in the moonlight under the oak and wanted to hear the fairy tales they had brought from the wide world. The owl told such wonderful things that no one wanted to go to sleep.

She put her fairy tales together like pearls on a string, and all the animals listened with bated breath. "How wise you are, Mrs. Owl!" Said a bear after the owl had finished. "I learned so much from you, it's too bad people do not know your fairy tales." The wise owl pondered the bear's words for a long time.

When she felt that she had not much time to live, she took a thick book and a quill pen. She wrote and wrote and wrote, and when she wrote the last story, she closed her eyes forever.But the thick book fell under the oak, and there I found it.

CPSIA information can be obtained
at www.ICGtesting.com
Printed in the USA
BVHW061356080221
599628BV00007B/492

9 781914 193941